Nishiguchi Essentials 100

Men's Fashion Director　　Shuhei Nishiguchi

メンズファッションディレクター
西口修平

INTRODUCTION

2020年に巻き起こった新型コロナウイルスの世界的大流行により、ステイホーム、ソーシャル・ディスタンシング、with マスクが当たり前に。私は洋服屋のひとりとして、このニューノーマルな時代において「生活必需品としての洋服ではなく、"自己表現のためのファッション"とどのように向き合うべきか」と考えるようになりました。そして見えてきた答えは、「これからも今までと変わりなく、自分らしいお洒落を楽しみ続けていきたい」という、素直な気持ちでした。私にとって"自分らしい"とは、モノ自体が持つ歴史やストーリー、そしてモノ作りの背景に敬意を表しながら、独自の解釈で現代的に落とし込んだスタイルのこと。本書では、そんな自分らしいスタイルを構成するうえで絶対に欠かすことができない、一生大切に付き合っていきたいと思えるアイテムを100点厳選しました。価値観が多様化したこの時代に、自身の心を震わすお気に入りのモノと出会い、それがスタイル・生き方を形成するうえで不可欠な存在になっていくのは、とても幸せなことだと思います。私が長年かけて培ってきた、モノの選び方・付き合い方のヒントを余すことなくお伝えしていきます。

メンズファッションディレクター　西口修平

With the pandemic of COVID-19 that broke out in 2020, stay home, social distances, and face masks have become our new normal. As a clothiers, I came to think in this new normal era, "How I should face and deal with fashion for self-expression rather than clothing as daily necessities?" The answer that came to me was a straightforward feeling, "I want to continue to enjoy my own fashion as I have always done." For me, "my own fashion" means my style that are modernized with my unique interpretations while paying homage to the history, stories, designs and manufacturing of items. In this book, I have carefully selected 100 items that I want to cherish for the rest of my life and absolutely indispensable for my own style. In this era of diversified values, I am very happy to meet my favorite items that shake my heart and become an indispensable part of shaping my style and way of life. I will give you all the tips on how to choose and interact with the items that I have cultivated over the years.

Men's Fashion Director　Shuhei Nishiguchi

CONTENTS   Nishiguchi
            Essentials
            100

page:

［西口式］
一生モノの選び方

[Nishiguchi style]
How to choose items
built to last a lifetime

Philosophy
（1）

歴史やストーリー性、
モノ作りの背景に共感できること

Being able to sympathize
with the history, stories,
and background of manufacturing.

Philosophy
（2）

例えひと目惚れだとしても
ずっと好きでいられる普遍性

Even if it's a love at first sight,
it has universality
that I can love forever.

Philosophy (3)

スタイリングのイマジネーションが
掻き立てられるデザインや色柄

Designs and colors
that arouse imaginations
of styling.

Philosophy (4)

修理して使い続けられる
素材や品質の高さ

High level of materials and quality
that can be repaired.

Philosophy (5)

購入時は分不相応でも
のちに似合うようになる可能性

Possibility to suit me better later,
even if it would not be suitable
at the time of purchase.

nᵒ 001
—
nᵒ 008

Watch & Jewelry

美しい手元、脱元は
女性陣の特権ではありません

"Beautiful hands and arms"
are not privileges only for women.

nº 001

ANTIQUE, SIGNATURE RING
アンティーク、シグネチャーリング

product : ring   made in England

material : 9k gold × diamond

100年の歴史を
子や孫の代まで受け継ぎたい

100 years of history to pass on
to my children and grandchildren.

約20年前、ロンドン留学していた友人が着けているのを見て以来、気になって探したのがアンティークのシグネチャーリングです。彼曰く「上流階級の人が、息子の成人の際に贈った」というエピソードを持つアイテム。ずいぶん昔の個体なので真偽は定かではありませんが、ゴールドの台座にダイヤモンドが小さく輝くその姿は、たしかに上品で貴族的。イギリスらしいイメージを凝縮したような美しい意匠に強く惹かれたのです。そして数年後、帰国した友人がそれをプレゼントしてくれました（写真右）。もう一方は私自身がロンドンのアンティークマーケットで見つけたものです。どちらも、もう少しで100年を迎える歴史あるジュエリーだけに、子や孫まで受け継いでいけるはず。長い年月でも劣化しにくい9金のゴールド製というのも、歴史の深さを物語ります。

Since I saw the antique signature ring worn by my friend who was studying in London about 20 years ago, I have been interested in signature rings and searched one for myself. My friend told me a story that a gentleman in upper class gave the ring to his son who became an adult man. It's a long time ago, so the truth is uncertain, but the appearance of a small diamond shining on a gold pedestal is certainly elegant and aristocratic. I was strongly attracted to the beautiful design, which seems to condense the British image. A few years later, my friend came back to Japan and kindly gave it to me as a gift. The other signature ring is the one that I found myself at an antique market in London. Both rings have history of almost 100 years, so they should worth to be handed down to children and grandchildren. The fact that they are made of 9K gold, which does not easily deteriorate over many years, shows the depth of history.

BREITLING,
CHRONOMAT
ブライトリング、クロノマット

product : watch   made in Switzerland

material : stainless steel

コロナ禍で気づかされた
時計の新たな価値

New values of the watches I found
under the COVID-19 pandemic.

2020年、私としては珍しく現行モデルを選びました。その理由は、何よりこの時計の持つ男らしい雰囲気が気に入ったから。新型コロナウイルスの影響から全世界的に自粛ムードが広がり、海外はもとより、街に出かけることさえ減った反動からか、車移動や公園などでのアクティブシーンで使えるスポーツウォッチが気になりはじめたのです。スポーツロレックスという選択肢がなかった私には、ケース径が44mmから42mmに小径化され、ブレスレットもクラシックな雰囲気のこのモデルは、ベストな選択。やや小振りになったとはいえラグジュアリーさと無骨さは兼ね備えているので、まさに男のための時計という佇まいです。Tシャツにジーンズといったラギッドで男らしいスタイリングにぴったりなので、いまや"新しい日常"には欠かせない相棒になりました。

In 2020, I bought a current model, which is unusual for me. I did so because I liked the manly style of this watch. Due to the COVID-19 pandemic, the mood of voluntary restraint has spread all over the world, and even going up to town is not welcomed. Probably due to counter reaction to these situations, I started to be interested in sports watches that can be used in active scenes such as driving cars and playing in parks. For me, who did not have a option to buy sporty Rolex, this model with a case diameter downsized from 44mm to 42mm and a classic bracelet was the best choice. Although it is a little small, it has both luxury and rugged style, which convinces me that it is a great watch for men. It looks perfect for rugged and masculine styling such as a T-shirt with a pair of jeans. It is now an indispensable friend to my "New Normal".

BULOVA,
1940S U.S. MILITARY 24HOUR
ブローバ、1940年代製 アメリカ軍 24 アワー

product : watch .... made in U.S.A. ....

material : case/stainless steel strap/nylon
....

出来の悪いヤツほど
愛おしい
Poorly built, but adorable.

第二次世界大戦中の1940年代にアメリカ軍官給品だった24時間計ウォッチは、潜水艦内などで昼夜がわからない場所でも時間を視認するために開発されたもの。ただ、本当に当時軍で支給されて普通に使えていたのかが疑わしいほど、とにかく時間が見にくい。それもなんだかとても愛おしく感じられるから不思議です。本来は戦闘用のラギッドな時計ですが、白黒のモノトーンダイヤルが私にはとてもモダンで都会的に映ります。より洗練させたいならブラック、ミリタリーテイストを押し出したい場合はカーキという具合に、ストラップの色次第で雰囲気も簡単に変えられます。カジュアル使いがメインですが、ラグジュアリーな装いのハズしとして使うこともしばしば。ラグジュアリーな服装にチープな時計を着けることを粋に感じる年齢になったのかもしれません。

In the 1940s under the World War II, this BULOVA military watch was developed and supplied for the U.S. Military. The 24-hour dial was developed in order for the submarine force to recognize time even under water where sunlight did not reach. It is so difficult for me to recognize time on this watch that I doubt if it was actually supplied to and used by the U.S. submarine force. Nevertheless, it's strange because I find it lovely. This is a rugged military watch for battlefield use, but to me, the black and white dial looks very modern and urban. You can change the watchband by yourself. I put a black watchband when I want more modern taste, and I replace it to olive one when I want more military taste. I wear this watch mainly with my casual items, as well as occasionally with my luxury items to have a little twist. Maybe I became old enough to find such twisted combination of luxury clothes with a cheap watch.

nº 004

BUNNEY, HANDMADE RING

バニー、ハンドメイドリング

product : ring .... made in England

material :
left/silver925 × 18k yellow gold
middle/silver925 right/18k yellow gold × 18k white gold

職人仕事はイギリスの
クラシック服さながら

Craftsmanship
just like British classic clothing.

アンティークジュエリー同様、完全なるハンドメイドで作られていること。
イギリスで1300年代から刻印されてきたホールマークを備え、信頼性
が高いこと。アンティークジュエリー愛好家の私としては、そういった
ストーリーに必然的に惹かれ、このシンプルで美しいリングに唯一無
二の価値を感じています。熟練の職人の手で生み出される最高品質の
地金を用いた素晴らしいジュエリーたちは、イギリスを発祥とするクラ
シックな洋服さながら。だからこそ、クラシックスタイルを着る人にと
っては、もっとも相性の良いジュエリーだと思います。ちなみにメンズ
ジュエリーは日本人には馴染みが薄いかもしれませんが、グローバル
においては、記念や誓い、祈りなどを込めて着けられるスタンダード
なアイテム。一生大切にするという誓いを込めて、着けていきたいです。

It is handmade like antique jewelry and highly reliable with the
hallmark that has been engraved in England since the 1300s. As an
antique jewelry lover, I am attracted to these stories, and I feel that
this simple and beautiful ring has a unique value not found in other
brands. The finest jewelry made from the highest quality bullions
produced by skilled craftsmen is just like classic English clothes.
That's why it's the best jewelry for those who wear classic clothes.
Men's jewelry may not be familiar to Japanese people, but globally, it
is common that men wear them with commemoration, vows, prayers,
etc. It is a ring that I would like to wear for the rest of my life.

nº 005

CARTIER,
1970S TANK LOUIS CARTIER LM
カルティエ、1970年代製 タンク ルイ カルティエ LM

product : watch　　　　made in Switzerland

material : case/18k yellow gold　strap/lizard

カジュアルスタイルでこそ
その真価は発揮される
True value shines in casual styles.

若い頃カルティエに対して漠然と抱いていたイメージは、どこか煌びやかで女性的なもの。しかし、デザインへの興味からタンクを調べていくと、その先入観は払拭されました。美しいデザインはたしかに女性的ですが、名前の由来通り戦車をイメージしたフォルムはあくまで硬派。100年以上変わらないデザインは、それほどまでに秀逸であるということの証といえます。無垢のケースに尖ったリューズのカボション、文字盤の6時位置にPARIS表記があるこちらは、1970年代に個人オーダーのみで販売されたモデル。顧客の腕に完璧に合わせた、サイズ調整の効かないDバックルが付属します。クラシックスタイルとの相性の良さはもちろんですが、この時計の真骨頂はカジュアルスタイルの時。私のような体育会系の男性でも、上品に見せてくれるのです。

When I was young, "gorgeous" and "feminine" were my vague images of Cartier. However, as I studied Tank from my interests in its design, such preconception was instantly erased. Although its simple and beautiful design is feminine, the form is actually very masculine, because it came from, as its name explains, a tank. The design remains unchanged for over 100 years, which proves that the watch is such perfection. This model has a solid case, a pointed crown with cabochon, and "PARIS" letters below VI on dial, which was sold only by personal orders in 1970s. It comes with a lizard leather watch band with a D-buckle perfectly fitted for its owner, which means that you cannot adjust the size of the band by yourself. It looks great with classic dress styles, needless to say. But you find its true value when you wear it in your casual style, making sporty guys like me look elegant, which is true attraction of the watch.

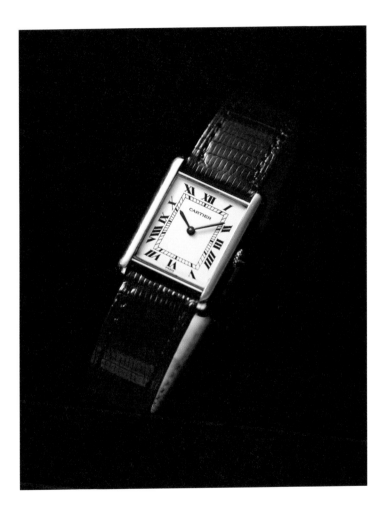

HERMÈS,
ANO TOUAREG H BANGLE

エルメス、アノー トゥアレグ H バングル

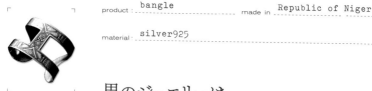

product : bangle   made in Republic of Niger

material : silver925

男のジュエリーは
傷が入っているくらいが粋

Men's jewelry becomes more tasteful
with scratches.

こちらは、1997年に発売されたl'Afriqueというコレクションの中のアノーというモデル。サハラ砂漠の遊牧民であるトゥアレグ族の職人がハンドメイドで作っていますが、同社のコレクションはその中でも高度な建築なども手がけるひと握りの極めて優秀な熟練の職人にしか制作が許されていないようです。今では結構メジャーになりましたが、購入当時はヨーロッパ出張に行くと業界の外国人が「それどこの?」「格好良いね!」と褒めてくれるひとつのコミュニケーションツールとして活躍してくれました。新品の洋服が恥ずかしいのと同様に、ジュエリーも新品だと自分に馴染んでないように感じて、最初は恥ずかしい気持ちになります。だから手入れはほとんどしていません。傷が多少入っているくらいの方が、男のジュエリーは粋に見えると思うのです。

This is ANO from the HERMÈS collection "l'Afrique" released in 1997. It is handmade by the craftsmen of the Touareg, nomads of the Sahara Desert. Only a handful of highly skilled craftsmen, who also handle advanced architecture, are allowed to work on HERMÈS collection, from what I heard. It has become quite famous now, but when I bought it and went on a business trip to Europe, many people in fashion industry talked to me like, "What is it?", "It's cool!". So it worked as a good communication tool. Just like you sometimes feel uncomfortable or ashamed in your new clothes, I feel the same when I put on new jewelry, feeling like it is not mine yet. That's why I haven't done much maintenance of it. I believe men's jewelry looks more tasteful after it gets some scratches.

OMEGA,
1960S DE VILLE CHRONOGRAPH
オメガ、1960年代製 デ・ヴィル クロノグラフ

product : watch .... made in Switzerland

material : case/18k plated × stainless steel
strap/crocodile
....

天邪鬼な一面が
自分自身に似ている

Its twisted style is similar to me.

デ・ヴィルとはフランス語で"街"の意味。その名が示す通り、街で着ける時計として小振りながらとても存在感があり、気に入っています。この時計はもともと知人が着用していたもので、私は優れたデザイン性に加え、知名度が高いスピードマスターではない点にも惹かれていました。「いつか」とその方にお願いしていて、のちに安く譲っていただいた思い出深い一本です。私の中でこのモデルの立ち位置は、上品な3針のドレスウォッチと精悍なメタルバンドのスポーツウォッチの中間。ドレススタイルをスポーティに仕上げたい時、カジュアルスタイルでは少しひねりたい時に重宝しています。男らしい3カウンターのクロノグラフにドレッシーなゴールドプレートケースという組み合わせも、どこか天邪鬼。自分に似ている気がして、妙に愛着が湧いてしまうんです。

"DE VILLE" is French for "city". As the name implies, it is a small watch for city use. I like this watch because it has a strong presence for its small size. Actually, this one belonged to my acquaintance. I like its design, as well as the fact that it is OMEGA but not a famous "Speedmaster". So I always asked him to pass it to me some day. Later, he kindly sold it to me cheap, which made this watch even more special to me. I think this watch is categorized in between elegant 3-hand dress watches and intrepid sporty watches with metal bands. I wear it in my dress styles, especially when I want to add a little bit of sporty taste. I also wear it in my casual styles, trying to add a small twist. I like the twisted combination of masculine 3-counter chronograph with dressy gold-plated case, because my character and styles are twisted, as well.

n⁰ 008

SWATCH,
1990S BLACK MOTION
スウォッチ、1990年代製 ブラックモーション

product : <u>watch</u>　　　made in <u>Switzerland</u>

material : <u>case/plastic　strap/leather</u>

悲しき別れを経て再会した
初恋の相手

My first love who came back
long after sad farewell.

女の子を意識して、お洒落をしたい! と思いはじめた頃に買ったの
が、1991年に発表されたスウォッチの自動巻き機種3型のうちのひ
とつ。現在は廃盤となったモデルです。この時計が登場したのは、
G-SHOCKやラバーバンドのスウォッチが全盛だった時代。当時のラバ
ーのスウォッチの相場は5～6千円ほどで、こちらは1万円くらい。16
歳の私には大きな出費だったのに、ひとつ年上の兄に貸した際、彼が
自転車で転んで風防が大破し、悲しみと怒りに打ちひしがれました。
実は写真は数年前にデッドストックを見つけ、買い直したもの。今では、
ミリタリーウォッチとは異なる、よりモダンなドレススタイルのハズしと
して使うことが多いですが、この時計を眺めるたびに当時の儚くも切
ない記憶が蘇ります。まるで初恋の相手ですね。

When I started to have interests in fashion with girls in mind, I
bought one of the three self-winding models of Swatch that were
released in 1991. This model is already discontinued. It first
appeared in the time when G-SHOCK or rubber-made Swatch were
so popular. While most rubber-made Swatch at that time cost about
5,000 to 6,000 yen, this one was about 10,000 yen, which was a big
expense for me as 16 years old. However, when I lent it to my older
brother, he fell off from his bicycle and the windshield of the watch
was wrecked. I was very sad and angry... So, the watch on the photo
is the one that I found and bought in dead stock condition a few
years ago. Now I mainly wear it as a unique accent in my dress style.
Every time I look at this watch, I remember the ephemeral memories
of those days. In that sense, this Swatch is like my first love.

n⁰ 009

---

n⁰ 025

Clothing（American）

古き良きアメリカモノも現代的に
私たちは現代人なのですから

Styling good old American items in modern ways,
because we live now.

BROOKS BROTHERS, BUTTON-DOWN SHIRT

ブルックス ブラザーズ、ボタンダウンシャツ

product : shirt _____ made in U.S.A. _____

material : cotton _____

定番たる所以は
美しい襟型にあり

The beautiful collar made the shirt
a classic standard.

言わずと知れたボタンダウンシャツの定番。その魅力は完成された襟型にあります。少しロングポイントで、自分でクセを付けることで変幻自在に好みのニュアンスを付けることが可能。洗い込むほどに柔らかく肌に馴染んでいくオックスフォード生地と相まって、無二の雰囲気を醸し出すのです。出会いは高校時代に訪れた古着店でしたが、当時はアメカジ全盛期だったためお洒落としてシャツを着る習慣がなく、購入には至りませんでした。その後、初めて袖を通すことになるのは、ドレスクロージングに興味を持ちはじめ、真面目にシャツを着ようと思いだした20歳の頃。そういう意味でこのボタンダウンシャツは、大人への第一歩を踏み出させてくれたシャツといえます。あれから20年以上経ちましたが、今でも私の定番として活躍してくれています。

Needless to say, this is a classic standard of button-down shirts. Its charm lies in the perfect collar. The beautiful collar with slightly long points allows you to add your favorite nuances. Combined with its oxford fabric, which becomes softer and more comfortable to your skin through repeated washes, it creates a unique style. I first met this shirt at a used clothing store when I was in high school. As it was the heyday of AMECAJI (American casual wear) in Japan, I didn't wear dress shirts as fashion. I didn't buy it. I was 20 years old when I first wore it. At that time, I started to have interests in dress clothing and decided to wear dress shirts as fashion. In that sense, this button-down shirt was my first step to becoming an adult. It's been over 20 years since then, and it's still a staple of mine.

CHAPS RALPH LAUREN, 1980S FIREMAN JACKET

チャップス ラルフ ローレン、1980年代製 ファイヤーマンジャケット

product : jacket   made in China

material : cotton

ドレススタイルのハズしとして使う
かなり変化球的なアイテム

A fairly unique item
used as a twist in dressy style.

カジュアルシーンでは何年かに一度登場するけれど、個人的にはスーツやジャケットに合わせたいと思わせるアイテム。そんな天邪鬼な洋服の代表格が、このファイヤーマンジャケットです。デニムにスニーカーで素直に合わせても良いのですが、それだとどうしてもアメリカの要素が強く出すぎることも。ラギッドなアイテムなので、テイストが真逆のドレス要素を加えて大人の装いを完成させています。特徴的なフロントのフック（ナスカン）はこのジャケットでしか見られないディテールで、緊急時に即座に留められる仕様として開発されたもの。機能のみを考えて作られた、究極のデザインです。ヴィンテージのリアルなファイヤーマンジャケットはいまだに探していますが、本物よりもラギッド感が少なく街着っぽく仕上がっている点にも面白さを感じます。

They appear once every few years in casual fashion scenes, but I personally want to match them with suits and jackets. Fireman jacket is one of such items to me. It's normal and totally fine to match it with denim and sneakers, but for me, that would make American taste too strong. As it is a rugged item, I match it with dressy items with the opposite tastes to complete a style for adult men. By the way, the front hook is a detail that can only be seen in this type of outerwear, and it was developed for firemen to immediately open or close the front in an emergency. I think it's the ultimate design, made with only functionality in mind. I'm still looking for a vintage, authentic Fireman jacket, but I find this jacket interesting that it's finished like a street wear with less ruggedness than professional fireman jackets.

GITMAN VINTAGE,
BUTTON-DOWN SHIRT

ギットマン ヴィンテージ、ボタンダウンシャツ

product : shirt   made in   U.S.A.

material : cotton

タイドアップするシャツとして
もっと認められるべき

It should be more recognized as a shirt
for tied-up styles.

タイドアップしたいけど少しラギッドに見せたい時に着ているのがこの
ボタンダウンシャツです。少しお坊ちゃんのイメージがあるブルックス
ブラザーズのものに比べて、ややラギッドで男臭いイメージ。襟型も
少し大きいためカジュアルな印象がありますが、吸い付くように登る台
襟とボディの完成度の高さから、佇まいはドレスシャツ然としています。
だから、個人的にはタイドアップするシャツとしてもっと認められるべ
きだと思っているんです。通常、アメリカ製のオックスフォード生地は
洗うほど目が詰まり硬くなりますが、着込んでいくうちに柔らかく馴染
んでくるのが特徴。ジーンズやレザーブルゾンなどと同様に、このシャ
ツにも"自分で育てる洋服"としての魅力が感じられます。ここのシャツ
にしかないダブルステッチの表情も、なんとも言えずたまりません。

I wear this button-down shirt when I want to wear a tie and look a
little rugged. Compared to Brooks Brothers shirts, which remind
of a preppy boy, it has a slightly more rugged and masculine style.
The collar is a little big, giving a casual impression. However, its
appearance is like a dress shirt, thanks to its collar nicely fit to
your neck and its perfectly patterned body. That's why I personally
think it should be more recognized as a shirt for tied-up styles. The
oxford fabric is made in the United States, and the more you wash it,
the harder it becomes due to clogging. Then, the more you wear it,
the softer and more comfortable it becomes, which is another feature
of this shirt. Like jeans and leather blousons, this shirt has the
same appeal as "clothes that you can raise by yourself". The double-
stitched look that is unique to this shirt is irresistible.

GOODWEAR,
HALF SLEEVE COLOR T-SHIRT
グッドウェア、半袖カラーTシャツ

product : t-shirt ---------------- made in U.S.A. ----------------

material : cotton ----------------

ニットのインナーとして
カラーTを使うと新鮮に見せられる

Color T-shirt under knitwear
for fresh look.

生地が分厚く質実剛健なTシャツ。首のリブ幅も太く、その土臭さが素晴らしい。着込むとリブ幅が横に伸びて少し細くなりますが、そのあたりから肌馴染みも良くなります。ボディよりも先に首のリブが破れてしまいますが、若い頃はそれも渋くてお気に入りでした。40歳を越えた今は、さすがに恥ずかしく感じるようになりましたが……。色物のTシャツを選んだ理由は、ウディ・アレンの影響が大きいと思います。彼がチェックシャツのインナーに着ているのは白ではなく微妙な色物で、それはあくまでさりげなく、でも作為的。まさに"ノンシャラン"の美学であり、自分自身のキャラクターを理解しているからこそ成せる技なのです。だから、私は彼と同じ着方はしません。自分らしく着こなすべく、シャツのインナーではなくニットのインナーとして使っています。

This is a T-shirt made of thick and solid fabric. The ribs on the neck are wide, leading to wonderfully earthy style. After wearing it several times, the ribs will stretch sideways and become a little slimmer, but from around that time the fabric will be softer and smoother to your skin. Normally, the ribs on the neck get torn earlier than the body. When I was young, I liked the look how the ribs on the neck got torn. Now that I'm over 40, I don't wear such a worn-out T-shirt. I think Woody Allen has a big influence on the reason why I wear colored T-shirts. What he wears under his checked shirts are not white, but they are normally subtle colors, which look casual but intentional at the same time. It's a "nonchalant" aesthetic, and it's a skill that can only be achieved by understanding your own character. So I don't wear a colored T-shirt in the same way as he does. Instead, I use it as an innerwear under knitwear for casual look.

HANES,
CREW NECK PACK T-SHIRTS JAPAN FIT

ヘインズ、クルーネック パック T シャツ ジャパンフィット

product : t-shirt .... made in China ....

material : cotton ....

インナーから下着へと
存在意義が変化する稀有なTシャツ

Rare T-shirts that transform
from inner clothes to underwear.

このTシャツは、初めのうちはジャケットなどのインナーとして、洗い込んで首周りが伸びてきたら下着として。付き合い方が変わっていく、私の中ではある意味、唯一無二の存在といえます。だからこそ、愛着を持って年中着ているのだと思います。実は、小学生の頃に初めて自分の小遣いで買ったTシャツも、ヘインズでした。当時はアメリカサイズのSでもブカブカでしたが、うれしくてたまらなかったのを覚えています。以来、長らくレギュラーフィットのものを着てきましたが、数年前にこのジャパンフィットが発売されてからは、ヘインズはこれ一筋ですね。スタイリングは、アメリカンテイストが強調されるようにジージャンやシャツのインナーにしたり、ローゲージニットの下に下着として着たりと様々。これからも末永く付き合っていく必需品です。

I first wear this T-shirt under my jackets. Then, after its neck is stretched out by repeated wearing and washing, I wear it as underwear. The relationship between this T-shirt and I changes, so in a sense, it's one and only T-shirt to me. That's why I love this T-shirt and wear it all year round. In fact, the first T-shirt I bought with my own money when I was an elementary school student was also Hanes. At that time, even the American size S was too big, but I remember I was so happy. I was wearing Regular Fit until the launch of this Japan Fit a few years ago. Since then, it has been my standard Hanes. I wear it under denim jackets and shirts as innerwear to emphasize American taste, and I also wear it under low gauge knitwear as underwear. It is my necessity, and continues to be so for many years to come.

LEVI'S,
501 JEANS
リーバイス、501 ジーンズ

product : jeans …………………………… made in U.S.A. ……………………………

material : cotton ……………………………………………………………………

20本以上所有して
なお欲しいと思わせる永世定番

Eternal classic.
Having more than 20 pairs already, not satisfied yet.

間違いなく、今までの人生で一番脚を通しているパンツ。1950年代XXから60年代のBigE、70年代66前期や80年代66後期、そして赤耳から90年代のレギュラー最後のアメリカ製まで、20本以上所有してなお欲しいと思わせる永世定番です。その"中庸さ"や"普通さ"ゆえ、洋服屋のあいだでは"リーバイスの501をお洒落に穿きなければ洋服屋じゃない"という言葉があるくらい、実はもっとも難易度が高いパンツとされています。現時点で私自身が穿きこなせているのかはわかりませんが、一生追求する価値のある最高のパンツという立ち位置は揺らぎません。どんなスタイリングにも寄り添ってくれるけれど穿く人のポテンシャルがそのまま現れる501は、活かすも殺すも自分次第。まさに"たかが洋服されど洋服"という言葉にふさわしいアイテムなのです。

Undoubtedly, Levi's 501 are the pants I've worn the most in my life. From the 50s "XX" to the 60s "Big E", the 70s early "66" and the 80s late "66", and from the "red selvage" to the 90s last US-made "regular", they are eternal classic jeans that make me want more, even after owning more than 20 pairs already. Among clothiers, there is a saying that "You are not a clothier if you cannot wear Levi's 501 stylishly". It is also said that they are the most difficult pants to wear stylishly. I don't know if I have been wearing them stylishly, but to me, Levi's 501 are definitely the best pants worth pursuing for a lifetime. The 501 are good for any styling. However, they expose the styling ability of the wearer. It is up to you whether you wear them well or not. It's an item that fits the phrase "It's just clothes, but it's still clothes".

LEVI'S, 70505-0217

リーバイス、70505-0217

product : trucker jacket

made in : U.S.A.

material : cotton

あえてドレススタイルに 取り入れるのが私流

It's my style to match it with dressy items.

高校時代に古着店で初めて購入したものはさすがに残っていません が、買い直しつつ20年以上愛用しているのがジージャンです。一番の 魅力は、なんといってもジーンズ並みにスタイリングの自由度が高いこ と。そのままカジュアルアイテムと合わせてももちろん良いのですが、 シンプルなドレススタイルに取り入れても面白い。私が以前から、"ジ ージャンはウールパンツを穿いてタイドアップするなどのドレススタイル にも合わせられるアイテムである"と提唱してきた結果、この業界でもリ バイバルを果たすこととなりました。テーラードのポロコートの中に着 るのも洒落て見えます。一方で、最近はあまり見かけなくなりましたが、 上下デニムでカジュアルなアウターを羽織るような、思いきりアメカジに 寄せた着こなしも、変わらず格好良いと思えるスタイルです。

I do not have the first one anymore that I bought at a used clothing store when I was a high school student, but I've had this model for over 20 years. The most attractive thing about this jacket is that it is as versatile as a pair of jeans. You can match it with casual items as everyone does, but it also looks good in simple elegant styles. I have always advocated that "Jean jacket can be well matched to elegant styles such as wearing wool pants and ties", and we have seen popularity revival of jean jackets in this industry. It looks fashionable when you wear it under a tailored polo coat. On the other hand, although I haven't seen this kind of style much these days, it's also a cool style when you match a jean jacket with a pair of jeans and a casual outerwear, to complete a straight American casual style.

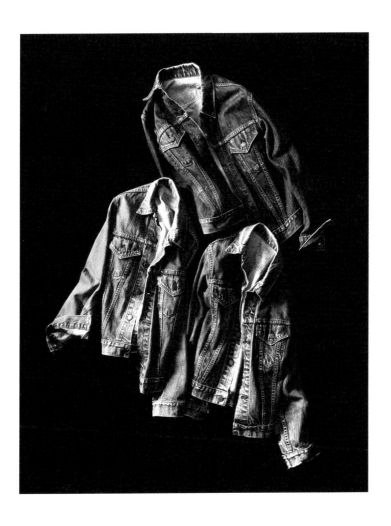

RALPH LAUREN,
1980-1990S TROUSERS
ラルフ ローレン、1980 ～ 1990年代製 トラウザーズ

product : trousers   made in U.S.A.

material : upper/cotton lower/wool

ラルフ・ローレン氏の魂を感じる
アメリカ製トラウザーズ

US-made trousers
that carry the soul of Mr. Ralph Lauren.

私は、1990年代の空気感がクラシックの世界にも影響を及ぼすことを予見し、2015年頃に2プリーツのチノパンを古着店で購入しました。当時はスリムシルエットしかほぼ売られていなかったため、買いたての頃は視覚的に慣れず「こんなに太いパンツをどう穿きこなしたらいいか」「90年代と同じようなバランスではなく現代的な着こなしとは」と試行錯誤したものです。所有しているこれらはすべて80 ～ 90年代のものですが、シルエットがとにかく太く、その当時の時代感を物語っています。所有しているアイテムを含め、ブランド全盛期のものはアメリカで作られているためラルフ・ローレン本人の魂が感じられますが、その後、残念ながらアメリカ製は姿を消してしまいました。個人的にはRRLが出る前の本物志向のMade in U.S.A.のものがお気に入りです。

Foreseeing that the 90s mood would affect the world of men's classic styles, I bought two-pleated chinos at a used clothing store in 2015. At that time, most of the pants in the market were slim pants, so the chinos that I bought were visually unfamiliar to me. "How should I wear these wide pants?" "What kind of styling would look more modern than the 90s with these wide chinos?" In order to find the answers to such questions, I remember trying various styling. All of these are from the 80s to the 90s, and their silhouettes are very wide, showing us the feeling of the times. Including the ones I own, Ralph Lauren's chinos from its prime time were US-made, and they tell us the soul of Mr. Ralph Lauren. Unfortunately, the US-made chinos already discontinued. Personally, I like the genuine US-made chinos before RRL came out.

RALPH LAUREN,
1990S TYPEWRITER TRENCH COAT

ラルフ ローレン、1990年代製 タイプライタートレンチコート

product : coat   made in   Singapore

material : cotton

上品な男らしさを備えた
1990年代の軽量コート

Elegant and masculine lightweight coat
from the 90s.

お洒落な先輩が着ているのを見てから探しはじめ、古着店巡りを数年続けた末にようやく出会ったのがこのタイプライタートレンチです。当時は"意地でも見つけてやる！"ということではなく、出会えたタイミングで買おうという感じでした。そんな風に思っていると、予想していないタイミングでふと現れるから、お店に足を運んで買い物をするのはやっぱりやめられません。そんなことを続けていたら、色違いで1着、形違いでまた1着という具合に、計3着も所有することに……。このコートの素晴らしさは、着ていることを忘れてしまうほどの軽さ。そして、ラギッドなイギリスブランド製のトレンチとは違い、上品な男らしさが感じられるところです。風になびく感じもこのコートならでは。ビッグボリュームと120cmほどの着丈も今の時代にはない良さだと思います。

After seeing my fashionable senior wearing it, I searched for it for several years at used clothing stores, and I finally met this typewriter trench coat. At that time, I wasn't like "I'll find it no matter what!", instead I was just like "I will buy it if I encounter it." Then, it suddenly appeared when I wasn't expected. This is why I can't stop going to stores for shopping. Later, I ended up owning 3 of them in total, one in different color and another one in different shape. The beauty of this coat is that it's so light that you forget you're wearing it. And unlike rugged British brands' trench coats, you feel elegant masculinity in it. The way it flutters in the wind is unique to this coat, too. I think its big volume and its length (about 120cm) are the features that you cannot easily find in current items.

□ Watch & Jewelry □ Clothing(American) □ Fashion Accessory □ Bag □ Clothing(European) □ Shoes □ Others

nº 018

RALPH LAUREN & RRL, SHIRT

ラルフ ローレン & ダブルアールエル、シャツ

product : shirt .... made in U.S.A. ....

material : cotton ....

クラシック好きのワードローブに
欠かせない万能選手

Essentials of classic style lovers' wardrobe.

ラルフ ローレンというブランドの魅力は、クラシックスタイルにおいて
あらゆるシーンに対応できる懐の深さ。シーズンごとにコンセプチュア
ルなコレクションで表現されていますが、クラシックの枠を超えない、
ブレない軸を持つ素晴らしいブランドだと思います。クラシック好きで
このブランドが嫌いな人はいないのではないでしょうか。また、生地
のバリエーションが幅広いのも魅力。今ではなかなか見つからないよう
な生地で作られているものが多く、スタイリングを引き立ててくれます。
私の中では、ブルックス ブラザーズやギットマンブラザーズはドレスの
イメージ、ラルフ ローレンはカジュアルのイメージが強いですが、その
分少年時代にも憧れ、40歳を超えた今でも素敵と思い続けられるブ
ランド。すべての世代に愛される、本当にすごい存在だと思っています。

Ralph Lauren collections are so versatile that you can wear them in
various scenes. It launches a conceptual collection for each season,
but I think it is a wonderful brand with a stable axis that does not
go beyond the boundaries of classic style. I mean, I believe there is
nobody who likes classic styles and doesn't like this brand. A wide
variety of fabrics are also the charm of this brand. Since there are
many items made of rare fabrics that are difficult to find today,
they can be great complement to your styling. I have impression
that Ralph Lauren produces great casual collections, while Brooks
Brothers and Gitman Brothers carry dressier collections. I longed
for Ralph Lauren as a little boy, and even now in the 40s, I still
think it is a wonderful brand and a truly amazing existence that is
loved by all generations.

THREE DOTS,
MERCERIZED T-SHIRT

スリードッツ、マーセライズ T シャツ

product : t-shirt   made in Japan

material : cotton

主役としても脇役としても活躍する
ラグジュアリーなドレスT

Luxury T-shirt that works
as both a leading role and a supporting role.

私がドレスTシャツに求める3つの条件は、❶透けないこと、❷型崩
れしにくいこと、❸1枚で着てもサマになるサイズバランスであること、
です。これらをすべて満たしているのがこのTシャツ。スーピマコット
ンを高密度で編み上げ、時間をかけて光沢を出すマーセライズと呼ば
れる加工を施した一枚は、しなやかなのにハリがあるのが特徴。ラグ
ジュアリーな雰囲気を備えた、まさにドレッシーなアイテムなのです。
もちろん、クルーネックニットをレイヤードしてチラリと見せても絵にな
ります。また、見た目の格好良さもさることながら、上質な素材を度
詰めしているため肌触りも素晴らしい。秋冬に下着のように着ても快適
です。主役として耐えうるよう手間隙を惜しまず作られたものだからこ
そ、脇役としても優れたパフォーマンスを発揮してくれます。

I set three conditions of an elegant T-shirt are (1) not to be
transparent, (2) to retain shape, and (3) to have a size and silhouette
that looks good when I wear it only. This T-shirt meets all of these
requirements. Supima cotton is knitted at a high density and
mercerizing processed over time to give it a luster, which gives soft
and elastic touch to the fabric. It's an elegant item with luxurious
vibes. Of course, even if you layer a crew neck knit pullover and
show the neck of the T-shirt, it looks good. In addition to its cool
appearance, its texture also feels great because it is knitted with
high-quality materials. It is comfortable to wear like underwear
in fall and winter. Because it was made with so much time and
efforts to be worn as a main item, it also demonstrates excellent
performance as a supporting item.

U.S. ARMY, 1950S M-51 MODS PARKA

アメリカ陸軍、1950年代製 M-51 モッズパーカ

product : ……field coat………………………… made in ……U.S.A.………………………

material : ……cotton × nylon……………………………………………………………

スーツに合わせる時には
ファーフードを外して

Remove the fur hood
when wearing it with a suit.

ザ・フーによるロックオペラ『四重人格』を原作とした1979年の映画『さ
らば青春の光』の影響で惚れ込んだ一着。1964年のロンドン、主人
公のジミー（フィル・ダニエルス）が、クラシックでタイトな3つボタン
のスーツにこのパーカを合わせた装いは、モッズがモダーンズの略であ
ることを体現するかのように、まさしくモダン。映画から学んだライニ
ングのボタンが外側から見えない留め方までいまだに実践しています。
また、劇中ではファーフードを付けずに着ていますが、これはスーツ
に対してファーが大袈裟に見えてモッズの美学に反するからなのでは?
などと推測するのも面白い。ちなみに、私が愛用している50年代のも
のは重量のあるウールパイルのライニング付きですが、M-65の中綿ラ
イニングの方が軽く洋服のシルエットが活きるため付け替えています。

"Quadrophenia" (1979), the movie based on the rock opera album
"Quadrophenia" by The Who, definitely influenced me and I fell in
love with this parka. London in 1964, the main character Jimmy
(Phil Daniels) looks very modern in his classic and tight 3 button
suit and this mods parka, as if he shows that the word "Mods" is an
abbreviation for "Moderns". From the movie, I learned how to button
the liner in the way the buttons are invisible. In the movie, Jimmy
wears this parka without the fur hood, and I guess it is because
the fur hood would look flamboyant to the suit and go against the
aesthetics of Mods. It's an interesting item that we can make such
guesses. My M-51 parka from the 50s comes with a heavy wool piled
liner, but I replaced it to the M-65 padded liner because it is lighter
and does not affect the silhouette of the parka.

U.S. ARMY,
1960S CHINOS
アメリカ陸軍、1960年代製 チノパン

product : <u>chinos</u> made in <u>U.S.A.</u>

material : <u>cotton</u>

ラギッドに見えながら
ドレス感を味わえる貴重なパンツ
Precious pants that look rugged yet
have a sense of elegance.

1941年に開発された戦闘服M-41の流れを汲むのがこの1960年代の
ヴィンテージチノです。ボタンフライからジッププライに変更され、50
年代に比べ少しだけテーパードが効いていて、穿いた時の腰周りのフ
ィット感が抜群。8.2オンスのコットンチノは洗ってもコシとハリがあり、
年を追うごとに自分の身体に馴染んでいくのを感じられます。このパ
ンツとのそもそもの出会いは大学生の頃。初めてアメリカ軍のヴィンテ
ージのチノパンを手にした喜びは、今でも鮮明に覚えています。当時
のチノパンはどこかにいってしまいましたが、しばらくしてから古着店
で見つけ、懐かしさのあまり思わず買い直しました。アメカジ一辺倒
だった学生時代とは違い、今では洗いざらしでもクリースを入れたり、
ヨーロッパスタイルに合わせたりと、自在に使いこなしています。

These vintage chinos are descended from the US Army combat
uniform M-41 that was developed in 1941. The button fly front
was replaced to zip fly front, and the legs were slightly tapered
compared to the 50s chinos. The fit around the waist is surprisingly
excellent. 8.2 ounce cotton chino fabric is firm to the touch and feels
like clothes that adapt to your body over the years. Actually, I first
encountered these vintage chinos when I was a college student. I
still vividly remember the joy of having my first US military vintage
chinos. I cannot remember where they are gone now, but after a while
I found the same chinos at a used clothing store and bought them
again with full of nostalgia. Unlike those days when I was only into
American casual, now I wear the chinos more freely, such as adding
creases even after washing and styling them in European style.

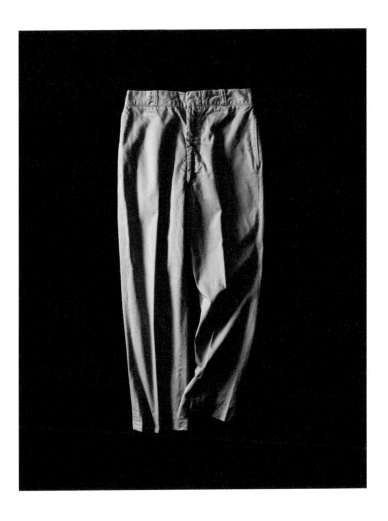

U.S. ARMY,
1970S M-65
アメリカ陸軍、1970年代製 M-65

product : ``field jacket`` .... made in ``U.S.A.``....................

material : ``cotton`` ....

あえて上品なスタイルに
羽織るのがお約束

I always dare to wear it
with elegant outfit.

M-65は、数々の名画の中で着用されてきました。『卒業』『ディア・ハンター』など挙げればキリがありませんが、やはり私の中では『タクシードライバー』のロバート・デ・ニーロの着こなしがNo.1。「モヒカンにM-65もありかも……」と思えてしまうほどです。もちろん実際はモヒカンにはしませんけど（笑）。デ・ニーロのようにハードボイルドな着こなしは私にはできません。テイストを合わせてカジュアルに着こなすというよりは、むしろ上品なスタイリングを程良く男らしく仕上げてくれるアウターという位置付けです。レギュラー丈のものを選べばジャケットの上から羽織った時にジャケットの裾が出ないという理由から、ヨーロッパの街角でもよく見かけますが、やはりクラシックを愛する男には外せないアイテム。世界一マストなアウターと言って過言ではありません。

The M-65 jackets have been worn in many movies. "The Graduate" and "The Deer Hunter" are just a few examples, but among them, Robert De Niro in "Taxi Driver" is the best for me. He looked so good in the movie that I thought, "Mohawk hair with M-65 jacket may be something I should try..." No, I won't make my hair Mohawk laughs. I can't wear M-65 jacket like De Niro did in the movie. I wear M-65 jacket as an outerwear that gives a moderately masculine finish to elegant styling, rather than wearing it casually. If you wear a regular length M-65 jacket on a tailored jacket, the hem of your jacket does not come out. Thus, M-65 jacket has been very popular in Europe, and it's one of the must-haves for men who love classic styles. It's not too much to say that it is the most famous outerwear in the world.

U.S. MILITARY, UNDERWEAR

アメリカ軍、アンダーウェア

product : underwear   made in : U.S.A.

material : upper/cotton
middle/cotton × polyester lower/cotton × wool

インナーでありながら
アクセント使いに好適

Underwear that is ideal
for style accents.

安い古着ばかりを買っていた大学時代。Tシャツや襟付きシャツ以外にインナー使いできるアイテムが何かないものかと探しており、辿り着いたのがミリタリーのアンダーウェアでした。素朴で肌馴染みの良いエクリュカラーや、現代の既製品にはないデザイン・素材感が面白く、インナーでありながら着こなしのアクセントになります。すべてが戦闘服の下に着ることを目的として作られたものだからこそ、身体へのフィット感が抜群で、着心地が良いのも魅力です。1978年のアメリカ映画『ディア・ハンター』では、主人公のマイケル（ロバート・デ・ニーロ）がサーマルのアンダーウェアをレイヤードしているシーンが格好良く描かれていて、「こんな風に自然体に着こなしたいなぁ」と思ったものです。大人が着るからこそヌケ感が醸し出せるアイテムだと思います。

I often bought cheap used clothes when I was in college. I was looking for underwear other than T-shirts and collared shirts, and I encountered military underwear. Simple and natural ecru colors, designs, and textures look interesting because they are different from modern ready-made clothes, and they can be good accent to your outfit. Because they were designed to be worn under combat uniforms, their fit are excellent and comfortable to wear. In the American movie "The Deer Hunter" 1978 that I saw a long time ago, the main role Michael Robert De Niro wears thermal underwear layered very naturally, which looks very cool. I thought "I have to wear them naturally like him." I think military underwear can add a sense of effortlessness especially when worn by the adults.

VINTAGE, 1990S BAND T-SHIRT

ヴィンテージ、1990年代製 バンド T シャツ

product : t-shirt
made in : upper/Republic of Honduras middle&lower/U.S.A.

material : cotton

唯一着るプリントTは 青春時代に熱狂したバンドモチーフ

The only print T-shirts I wear are those of rock bands
I got crazy about in my youth.

中学時代に、初めてガンズ・アンド・ローゼズやアイアン・メイデンを聴いて以来、私のヘヴィメタル好きは始まりました。中高生の頃をピークに好きだったガンズやメタリカは、私の青春そのもの。今はジャズがメインですが、それでも時々、車の中で聴いています。バンドTを着るようになったのは、ここ数年のこと。「長年慣れ親しんできたカルチャーを、自分の中にしっかり残しておきたい」「好きなモノを身にまといたい」という思いが年齢を重ねるごとに強くなってきたからです。だから、大好きなバンドのTシャツで、プリントも好みのものだけを厳選しています。ライダーズと軽めのローファーを合わせたり、夏は細いジーンズとサイドゴアブーツで上品に味付けしたりと、"洒落"で着ているように見せるテクニックを駆使しつつ、さりげなく楽しんでいます。

My love for heavy metal music has started when I first heard Guns
N' Roses and Iron Maiden when I was a junior high school student.
Guns N' Roses and Metallica, which I loved the most when I was in
junior high and high school, are my youth itself. Nowadays, I listen
to jazz the most, but sometimes I listen to heavy metal in my car.
It was a few years ago when I started to wear band T-shirts. This
is because my desires to "keep my all-time favorite culture in me"
and to "wear what I like" became stronger as I got older. That's why
I only wear my favorite print T-shirts of my favorite bands. I enjoy
them casually, while making full use of the techniques to make it
look like I'm wearing them as fashion, such as matching a rider's
jacket and light loafers, and wearing slim jeans and side-gore boots
in summer for elegant look.

WRANGLER,
1970-1980S WESTERN SHIRT
ラングラー、1970 ～ 1980年代製 ウエスタンシャツ

product : shirt   made in U.S.A.

material : cotton

ラルフ・ローレン氏の
着こなしのその先に

Mr. Ralph Lauren's style
and stepping forward from it.

下に長く伸びたレギュラーカラー、装飾性の高いカッティングやドット
ボタン……。特に1980年代以前の襟型は美しく、一方で生地は硬く
分厚くタフ。アメリカ西部の歴史が生んだ荒々しくもどこかドレスの匂
いのする、まさに男前なシャツです。私は、ラルフ・ローレン氏がこ
のシャツをクラシックスタイルに合わせている資料を見て魅了されまし
た。今となってはごく自然な着こなしなのですが、ヴィンテージや古着
をクラシックスタイルに取り入れることを誰もやっていなかった80年代
としてはかなり斬新といえます。常に新しい着方や洋服の可能性を追
求している私には、かなり魅力的に映ったのです。コーディネートに関
しては、ジャケットはもちろん、カジュアルなスーツに着たり、タイドア
ップしたりするのも面白いと思います。上質なテーラードアイテムで合
わせてこそ、ヴィンテージのウエスタンシャツの良さが活きるのです。

Long-pointed regular collars, highly decorative cutting, and dot
buttons ... The collars of these shirts, especially from the 80s
or before, are beautiful, and the fabrics are harder and thicker.
Originated from the western United States, they are manly shirts
that look wild yet slightly dressy. I was fascinated by the way
Mr. Ralph Lauren wears this shirt with classic dress items in a
photography I saw. It's pretty common now, but it's very innovative
in the 80s when incorporating vintage and used clothing into
classic style was something no one else was doing. I always pursue
new ways of dressing and possibilities of clothes, and his style
looked so novel and attractive. As for styling, they look great with
tailored jackets or casual suits. It's also fun to wear them with ties.
The goodness of vintage western shirts stands out even more when
matched with quality tailored items.

nº 026

—

nº 041

Fashion Accessory

足したり 引いたり 残したり
目指すは ノンシャランとした 佇まい
Add, subtract, or leave it,
aiming for a nonchalant appearance.

ALBERT THURSTON, BRACES

アルバート サーストン、ブレイシーズ

product : braces .... made in England ....

material : polyester × polyurethane ....

ドレスクロージングの門を
叩いた時に買った思い出の品

Memorable item that I bought
when I started my career in dress clothing.

股上が深いトラウザーズに使用すると、ヒップラインが吊られることで
シルエットを最大限に美しく見せてくれるアイテム。ベルトがまだなか
った時代の紳士の小道具らしく、装飾性が高いのもポイントです。欧
米では元来、人前でジャケットを脱がないのがマナーとされています。
だから当然、このブレイシーズも人目に触れないもの。にもかかわらず、
そこに色や柄を用いているという点に、イギリスらしい奥ゆかしさを感
じます。ちなみに、初めてブレイシーズを購入したのは、私がドレス
クロージングの門を叩いた約20年前。ストラップにクジラの髭が使わ
れた、今となっては稀少性の高いものでしたが、ほとんど使わないう
ちに失くしてしまいました。後悔している反面で、あの頃からブレイシ
ーズが似合う大人になりたいという思いは、ずっと変わっていません。

When the braces are used for trousers with a deep rise, the hip line
is hung to make the silhouette beautiful. Braces were gentleman's
prop when there was no belt yet, and it is notable that they were
decorative. In Europe and the United States, social etiquette
dictates that men cannot take off jackets in public. This means
that the braces are usually invisible in public. Nevertheless, the
braces have various patterns and colors, which I think is a sense of
British elegance. By the way, I first bought braces about 20 years
ago when I started my career in men's dress clothing industry.
Whale beards were used on the straps, which are now rare. But I
lost them before I used them much. While I regret that I should
have kept them, my desire to become a man who looks good on
braces hasn't changed since then.

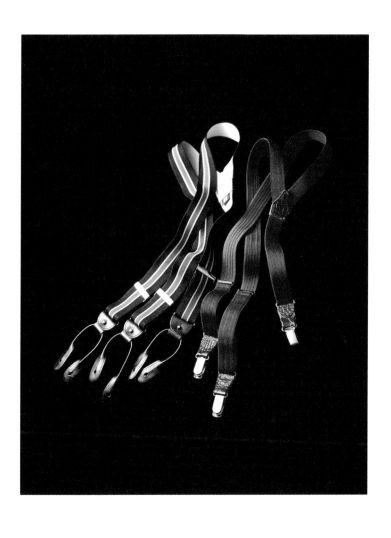

ALGHA WORKS,
1960S GLASSES

アルガワークス、1960年代製 眼鏡

product : glasses .... made in England

material : 14k rolled gold ....

賢くない私でも不思議と
賢そうに見える金縁の眼鏡

Gold-rimmed glasses that make even
a guy like me look intelligent.

限りなくシンプルで美しく、主張がない。かけ心地が良く、視界も広い。意匠としても道具としても最高傑作だと思える金縁の眼鏡です。フルビューといわれる玉型で、高い位置にテンプルがあるのが特徴。14金を幾重にも重ねたロールドゴールドのフレームは、何年使用しても金が剥がれず、製作から60年ほど経った今も色褪せない魅力を放ちます。実は、私の視力は裸眼で1.5。視力矯正の道具としては必要ありませんが、眼鏡で自分のイメージを変えたり、洋服の雰囲気を変えたりできることに気づいてから収集しはじめました。その中でもよく使うのがこの一本。ゴールドのジュエリーを着けることの多い私には自然と馴染むアイテムです。ヨーロッパの洋服で構成する時、少し堅いスタイリングにとても相性が良く感じるのは、イギリスの眼鏡だからなのでしょうね。

These are glasses of infinitely simple, beautiful, and unassertive
designs. They are comfortable to wear and have broad visual field.
In my opinion, these gold-rimmed glasses are a masterpiece both
as design and as a tool. It features a lens shape called full view
and a temple at high positions. The rolled gold frames, which are
made of 14K gold layers, do not come off even after many years of
use. Even now, about 60 years after its production, they still have
fascinating appeal. Actually, I have 20/13 vision without glasses,
so I don't need glasses as a vision correction tool, but I started
collecting them when I realized that I could change my image and
the styles of my clothes with them. These glasses are the ones that
I wear the most among them. I often wear gold jewelry, so I can
style these glasses more naturally than others. I feel that these are
good match with slightly conservative and dressy styling, which I
think it's because they are British glasses.

◻ Watch & Jewely

◻ Clothing/American

◻ Fashion Accessory

◻ Bag

◻ Clothing/European

◻ Shoes

◻ Others

AMERICAN OPTICAL,
1930S GLASSES & CLIP-ON SUNGLASSES
アメリカン オプティカル、1930 年代製 眼鏡＆クリップオンサングラス

product : glasses & clip-on sunglasses　made in　U.S.A.

material : 12k gold filled

見た目は格好良いのに
完璧じゃないのも魅力

Not perfect but still stylish and charming.

眼鏡の歴史を調べると必ず出てくるのが、このアメリカン オプティカル
です。眼鏡の歴史を作ってきたブランドと言っても過言ではない存在
ゆえに、いつかは手に入れたいと思っていました。眼鏡の装飾のため
に彫金師を自社に雇い入れたり、乗馬中の眼鏡の落下を防ぐために
耳位置でツルを半月に曲げたり、メッキが落ちにくいよう厚い12金張り
（12KGF）を施したりと、当時の技術が徹底的に注がれているところに
男心をくすぐられます。イギリスのアルガワークスの眼鏡を購入してから、
よりクラシカルなものを探し求めてこのモデルに辿り着きました。また、
同じタイミングで入手した同年代のクリップオンサングラスには当時の
ガラスレンズが入っていたのですが、付けると重すぎて前にズレるんで
す。見た目は格好良いのに完璧ではないところにも、愛着を感じます。

If you study the history of eyeglasses, you will definitely know
American Optical. It is not too much to say that this is the brand
that made the history of eyeglasses, so I had wanted to own its
glasses. It hired goldsmiths to decorate eyeglasses, bent the temples
in half-moon shape at the ear position to prevent the glasses from
falling on horseback, and applied a thick 12K gold plating (12KGF)
to prevent the plating from peeling off. Cutting-edge technologies
at that time were thoroughly applied to produce innovative glasses,
which tickles men's hearts even today. After I had purchased the
glasses of Algha Works in England, I bought this model in search
of something more classical. I also bought clip-on sunglasses with
original glass lenses from the same age, but if I wear them, they
slip forward along my nose because they are too heavy. They look
great, but not perfectly built, which is charming.

BORSALINO,
FELT HAT

ボルサリーノ、フェルトハット

product : hat........................... made in Italy.........................

material : rabbit fur felt................ ....

スタイルへ落とし込むのに
時間を要する男の小道具

A man's prop that requires some time to
naturally fit to your style.

『ゴッドファーザー』などのマフィア映画が若い頃から大好きでした。スーツ&フェルトハットというスタイリングを好むようになったのは、そういった映画の世界観への憧れからだと思います。「自分のスタイルに落とし込むのに時間を要する」とわかっていたため、30代では小生意気に見えてしまうことを重々承知で、あえて早くから実践してきました。ハットは、ブリムのクセ付けや被る角度、所作なども含め、時間をかけてこそモノにできる男の小道具。まだ早いと知りつつ当時から被り続けた経験は、今に活きていると思います。この最高級のラビットファーフェルトは、軽く、被り心地が良く、クラウンの形状も実にエレガント。格別のオーラをまとった主役級のアイテムです。年齢を重ねながら、ますますこのハットが似合う男になりたいですね。

I've loved mafia movies such as "The Godfather" since I was young.
I think that I came to like the styling of suits and felt hats because
of my longing for such movies. I knew that it would require some
time for me to fit a felt hat to my own style, so I dared to start
wearing it from my thirties, even though I knew that it would look
cheeky. A hat is a man's prop that requires some time to make it
truly yours, including the process of shaping the brim, finding
the best angle to wear, and learning manners and behaviors. I kept
wearing it, while I knew it was too early for me. Such experiences
are now rewarded. This finest rabbit fur felt is light, comfortable to
wear, and has a truly elegant crown shape. It is an item of leading
role grade with a special aura. As I get older, I want to become a
man who looks better with this hat.

COACH,
1990S NARROW BELT
コーチ、1990年代製 ナローベルト

product : belt .... made in U.S.A. ....

material : cowhide leather ....

ブランドの原点ともいえる
グローブレザー製の細幅ベルト

Where it all started:
the narrow belt made of glove leather.

丁寧に鞣された肉厚のカウハイドレザーは、使い込むほどに味わいが
増していくグローブレザーと呼ばれるもの。現在、オールドコーチのバ
ッグがヴィンテージの市場で有名になっていますが、このベルトには
それらと同様の革が使用されています。また、クラシックの世界では、
ベルトの幅は30〜35mmがセオリーとされていますが、こちらはより細
めの25mm。細幅のベルトは時代感を演出でき、少しゆったりとしたシ
ルエットのスタイリングにとても重宝します。現代的でありながら、美
しい縫製や真鍮製のバックルが実にクラシックな雰囲気で、細幅でも
フェミニンに見えません。まさに自分が求めるイメージにぴったりの一
本です。良質なレザーと、細部に行きわたったクラフトマンシップを
味わえる、コーチの原点ともいえる名品だと思います。

This carefully-tanned thick cowhide leather is called glove leather,
and its color will gradually change over time and have more depth
as you use it. Old COACH bags are now well known in the vintage
market, but this belt is made of similar leather as those belts. In
the world of classic clothing, the width of the belt typically ranges
from 30 to 35 mm, but the width of this belt is 25 mm. The narrow
belt can create a sense of the times and is very useful when styling
a slightly loose silhouette. Very modern, yet beautiful sewing
and its brass buckle give it a truly classic feel, and it doesn't look
feminine It's very easy to style and exactly my image of an ideal
belt. With high quality leather and careful craftsmanship, it is
definitely a masterpiece, telling what COACH is all about.

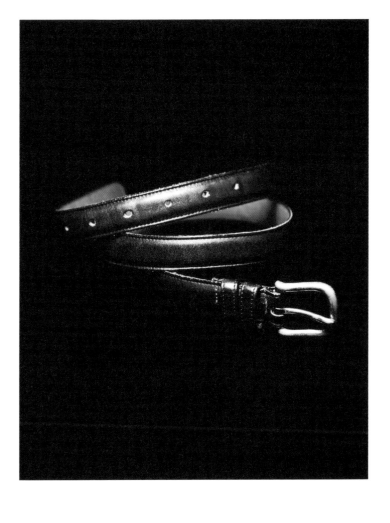

E.MARINELLA, PRINT TIE

マリネッラ、プリントネクタイ

product : tie   made in Italy

material : silk

美しい曲線を描くノットは
E.マリネッラならではの魅力

The beautifully curved knots are unique charm of
E. Marinella ties.

クラシックスタイルを愛する者にとって、いつかは必ず手に入れたいと思えるネクタイブランド。セッテピエゲと呼ばれる7つ折りされた幅広のネクタイは、熟練職人の伝統的な技術により手縫いで仕上げられます。イギリス製のヘビーなシルクのプリント生地と厚手の芯地によるノットの美しい曲線は、このブランドならでは。何度締めていても生地にハリがあり、シワがすぐに回復することにも驚かされます。使い込めば使い込むほどシルクがしなやかになり、ぬめり感が出てくると、さらに締めやすくなるのが本当に素晴らしい。生産本数は1種類の柄あたり数本のみと限られているので、気に入る柄があったら迷わず購入することをオススメします。実にイタリアらしくエレガントなネクタイだと思っているので、ナポリ仕立てのスーツやジャケットと合わせることが多いですね。

For those who love classic styles, this is a tie brand that everyone dreams to buy some day. The wide seven-folded tie, called the sette pieghe, is hand-sewn using traditional techniques by skilled craftsmen. The beautiful curves of the knots made of heavy silk print fabric made in England and the thick interlining cloth is the charm of this brand. No matter how many times you tie it, the fabric remains resilient, and you will be surprised that the wrinkles recover quickly. The more you use it, the suppler and sleeker the silk becomes and the easier it is to tie. The number of ties produced is limited to only a few per pattern, so if you find a pattern you like, I recommend you to purchase it without hesitation. I personally think that it is a very Italian tie, so I often style it with a Napoli-made suit or jacket.

nº 032

ETRO,
PAISLEY SCARF
エトロ、ペイズリー柄マフラー

product : scarf   made in Italy

material : silk × cashmere

恩師から譲り受け20年の時を経て
似合うようになってきた

After 20 years since my teacher gave it to me,
it finally suits me.

ハンドプリントのシルクペイズリーと最高級のカシミアがリバーシブル
になったマフラーは、大学時代の恩師から卒業記念にいただいた大
切な品。大学の講義で出会った恩師はとてもお洒落で、キートンのス
ーツに足元はエドワード グリーンという出で立ちでした。そのあまりに
も完璧なスタイルに、お会いした当日に不躾ながら声をかけさせてい
ただいて……。それから、洋服を共通言語にして食事をご一緒するな
ど、常にご恩を感じていた憧れの存在です。恩師から「もう使わない
から」とこの品を譲り受けた当時は、「自分にはまだ早い」と思ってい
ました。でも、あれから20年が経って、ようやく少しは似合う年齢に。
歳を重ねるほどに似合うようになるものなので、今思えば、あのお言
葉は贈り物だと気づかせないための粋な計らいだったのでしょうね。

The hand-printed silk paisley and the finest cashmere reversible
scarf is my treasure that my teacher in college gave me to
commemorate my graduation. I first met this gentleman at a
lecture in my university. On the day I first met him, he dressed
himself in his Kiton suit and Edward Green shoes. I could not
help talking to him about his perfect style. Then, we talked about
clothes over lunch and dinner together a few times. I feel really
grateful and respectful to him. When I received this scarf from the
teacher, he only said to me, "I don't use it anymore." And I thought
I was too young to wear this scarf. However, 20 years passed, and
I've finally reached an age that the scarf looks better on me. Now
I believe what he said to me was his thoughtful technique not to
make me realize it was a gift to me.

□ Watch & Jewelry

□ Clothing/American

□ Fashion Accessory

□ Bag

□ Clothing/European

□ Shoes

□ Others

HERMÈS, CARRE

エルメス、カレ

product : scarf　　　　　made in France

material : silk

芸術品のようなオーラを
胸元で放ち続けるファースト・エルメス

My first Hermès continues to give off an aura
like a work of art on my chest.

20年以上前、ドレスクロージングに身を置くようになってから、ふら
りと立ち寄ったヴィンテージショップで出会ったのがベージュのカレ。
既製品とは思えないほど絶妙な色で表現された、絵画のように美しい
柄に惹かれて衝動買いしました。これが私のファースト・エルメスです。
何重にも塗り重ねられたシルクスクリーンのプリント、重くぬめりのあ
る最高級のシルクツイル、手縫いで縫製されたハンドロールヘムと呼
ばれる端の処理……。どの要素をとっても、芸術品と言っても過言で
はないクオリティです。また、一般的なスカーフとは表裏逆の、表に
ロールが出る通称"エルメスロール"も粋。胸元に挿すと見える面積は
ごくわずかですが、その儚さも素敵です。狭い面積でもオーラが強い
ため、全体の装いでカレに負けないように心がけています。

More than 20 years ago, soon after I started my career in dress
clothing, I met this beige Carré at a vintage shop that I stopped
by. I bought it on impulse because I was attracted to the beautiful
pattern like a painting, which was expressed in exquisite colors
that I couldn't think of as an off-the-shelf product. This is my first
Hermes. Multi-layered silkscreen prints, heavy, sleek, finest silk
twill, and hand-sewn edge treatments called hand roll hem... It is
not an exaggeration to say that any element is a work of art. In
addition, the so-called "Hermes roll", a roll on the front side which
is the opposite of other general scarves, is also stylish. The area
you can see when you insert it on your chest pocket is very small,
but its subtleness is also wonderful. Even in a small area, the aura
of the Carré is strong, so I try to balance my overall outfit so that
it does not look too showy.

J EYEWEAR LAB × OPTICAL KILICO, BESPOKE GLASSES

ジェイ アイウエア ラボ × オプティカル・キリコ、ビスポーク眼鏡

product : glasses　　　　　　　　made in　England

material : acetate

ドレススタイルで合わせたくなる
背筋の伸びる眼鏡

Neatly dressed,
it straightens up my back.

ブラウンのセルフレームは何本か所有していたものの、その中からしっくりくる一本を選べない時期がありました。眼鏡のビスポークを知ったのは、ちょうどその頃。知人が職人さんを紹介してくれたのですが、初めての眼鏡のオーダーはとても貴重な経験となりました。自分の理想を具現化するべく、もちろんフレームはブラウンをチョイス。60年代のイギリス製のデッドストックのアセテート素材の塊を削り出して成型したものです。デザインは、1948〜85年にイギリスの保健制度「NHS」によって国民に支給された「NHS SPECTACLE」という眼鏡がベース。ウエリントン型ながら華奢で、アメリカモノよりも主張がやや控えめなのは、お国柄なのかもしれません。きっちりとしたドレススタイルに合わせたくなる、"背筋の伸びる眼鏡"に仕上がりました。

I owned several brown plastic frame eyeglasses, but there was a time when I couldn't choose the ones that suit me best. It was around that time that I learned about bespoke glasses. An acquaintance introduced me to a craftsman, and it became a very valuable experience for me to order eyeglasses for the first time. Of course, I chose brown for the frame to realize my ideal. It was made by carving out a block of acetate which is the 60s dead stock material from the UK. The design is based on the "NHS SPECTACLE" glasses, which were provided free of charge to the public by the NHS, British public-health service from 1948 to 1985. The shape is categorized as so-called "Wellington-style", but these look more delicate and a little more modest than the same style of glasses from the US. This eyewear straightens up my back, and I want to put them on with a neat dressy outfit.

J&M DAVIDSON, RING BELT

ジェイ ＆ エム デヴィッドソン、リングベルト

product : belt

made in Spain

material : cowhide leather

上手く着けこなせるか否かを
試されているような気がするベルト

A belt that seems to test me
if I can style it well or not.

20㎜幅のリングベルトは、ユニセックス商品ながらサイズ展開がワン
サイズのみ。この潔い作りは、素直に解釈すれば「どうぞ自由に着け
てください」というメッセージ。しかし、天邪鬼な私としては「どうぞ
お洒落に着けられるものなら着けてみなさい」という挑戦状のように
も思え、「受けて立とう！」とばかりにコーディネートの可能性を探りた
くなります。このベルトの一番の魅力は、しなやかで女性的な印象と、
力強く男性的な印象が違和感なく同居している点。幅はスリムながら、
革は質実剛健なのです。私にとっては、ドレス感とカジュアル感をバ
ランス良く構成する際のつなぎ役のような存在といえます。なお、華
奢でありながら存在感のあるベルトなので、極力シンプルなスタイリ
ングにすることでベルトが嫌味に見えないようにしています。

This 20mm wide ring belt is a unisex product, and it's free size.
This should mean, "Please wear this belt as you like.", if you
interpret it straightly. However, to me, with a twisted personality,
it seems like a challenge like, "Do you have the ability to wear
this belt fashionably?" I want to explore the possibilities of
coordination, so I say "I take the challenge." The most attractive
point of this belt is that it has a supple and feminine impression
and a strong and masculine impression without any discomfort.
The width is narrow and delicate, but the leather is simple and
sturdy. For me, this belt is like a linker, balancing elegance and
casualness. The belt is slim yet has a strong presence, so I style
myself as simple as possible so that the belt doesn't look ugly.

LAULHERE, BERET

ローレル、ベレー帽

product : beret ---------------------------------- made in France ----------------------------------

material : wool ---

シンプルで品のあるスタイリングを
小気味良く仕上げる名脇役

A good supporting role that smartly completes
a simple and elegant style.

ベレー帽は、単体でなんとなくお洒落に見せることができるアイテム。だからこそ、若い頃から漠然と「ごまかしの効かないシンプルなスタイリングが可能な年齢になってからトライしよう」と思っていました。様々な洋服を着て自分を表現するうちに、40歳の頃、「このスタイリングにはベレー帽をプラスした方がもっと良くなるのでは」と感じるようになったのです。ベレー帽といえば、どうしてもフランスっぽいイメージが強いかもしれません。しかし私は、装いに関係なく合わせています。ベレー帽の本領が発揮されるのは、ドレスやカジュアルを問わず、どこか品のあるスタイリング。装いになんともいえない小気味良さを生むのです。なお、マナー違反であることは重々承知していますが、室内で脱がなくても抵抗を感じさせない手軽さも気に入っています。

A beret is an item that can easily make you look fashionable by itself. That's why, from a young age, I vaguely thought, "I'll try it when I'm old enough to look good even if I wear simple outfit." I think I wear wider ranges of clothes than others, and as I try various styles, I came to feel, "I think it would be better to add a beret to this style.", when I was 40 years old. Speaking of berets, you may have a strong image of France. But I do not care much about it when I wear it. The true value of the beret is found when it is worn in a style with some sort of elegance, no matter it is a dressy style or casual style. Besides, even if we do not take off berets indoor, people do not feel uncomfortable. That is also why I like berets, although it is a bad manner.

RALPH LAUREN, VINTAGE TIE

ラルフ ローレン、ヴィンテージネクタイ

product : tie ----------------------------------- made in U.S.A. ---------------------------------

material : silk --

コスト度外視で作られた
極上の大柄プリントが洒脱

The finest large pattern print
that was made ignoring the cost.

ラルフ・ローレン氏はデザイナーとしてのキャリアをネクタイのデザイン
からスタートしました。その経歴からもわかる通り、創業から1990年
代にかけてのラルフ ローレンのプリントタイへの力の入れようは相当な
もの。当時のネクタイデザイナーが起こしたプリントタイには大柄で大
胆なものが多いのも特徴です。大柄であればあるほどシルク生地の取
り都合が悪くなるためコストがかかりますが、それでも良いデザイン
を描きたいという信念が窺えます。シルクスクリーンを何度も重ねて
仕上げるプリントのクオリティも素晴らしい。そんな手間暇をかけてハ
ンドメイドされたネクタイが、いまや貴重なアメリカ製というところもお
気に入り。芯地も極力薄いもので構成されているため、プレーンノット
を限界まで小さく結ぶという私のスタイルを実現できます。

Ralph Lauren started his career as a tie designer. As you can
imagine from this fact, Ralph Lauren's efforts in print ties
especially until 1990s were considerable. Many of the print ties
from this period had large and bold patterns. The larger the
pattern is, the more difficult it gets to make more ties out of silk
fabric, which means the rise of the cost. What we can see from
the large patterns of the ties is the brand's dedication to quality
tie designs even if it gets costly. The quality of the print, which
is finished by layering silk screens many times, is also excellent.
I also like the fact that these ties were handmade in the United
States, which is rare now. Since the interlining is made of very
thin fabric, I can make my plain knot as small as possible.

SIMONNOT-GODARD,
POCKET SQUARE

シモノ ゴダール、ポケットチーフ

product : pocket square   made in France

material : cotton

クラシックな男の胸に
ひっそりと寄り添う美しいチーフ

A beautiful pocket square that snuggles up to
the chest of a classic man.

シモノ ゴダールは、エルメスから生産を任されるほど優秀なコットン
チーフ専業メーカー。コットンの素材が素晴らしく、さらにハンドロー
ルヘムと呼ばれる端の処理も最高に美しい。世界一端整なコットンの
ハンカチといって良いでしょう。実に上品で、クラシックな男の胸にオ
ーラをそっと添えてくれます。90年代後半に購入して以来(写真中)、
日本国内で見かけることが少なくなっていましたが、十数年前に、今
はなきフィレンツェの名店「タイ ユア タイ」で発見(写真左・右)。お
店で「コットンやリネンのチーフを見せて欲しい」とリクエストすると、
バックヤードからたくさん出して見せてくれました。「やはり、良いお店
には良いモノが置かれているのだな」と感動したものです。もしかし
たら売れ残りだったのかもしれませんが……(笑)。

Simonnot-Godard is an excellent cotton handkerchief manufacturer
that is entrusted with production by Hermès. The cotton material
is excellent, and the edge treatment called the hand roll hem is
also very beautiful. I can say that it is the most beautiful cotton
handkerchief in the world. It's really elegant and quietly adds an
aura to the chest of a classic man. Since I bought it in the latter
half of the 90s (the one in the middle in the picture), I had rarely
seen it in Japan, but I found it at the now-defunct Florence's famous
store "Tie Your Tie" more than ten years ago (left and right in the
photo). At the shop, I asked "I would like to see pocket squares of
cotton or linen." A store staff brought me a lot of them from the
backroom. I was impressed and thought, "It's true that a good store
sells good stuff." Or it may be just that they were left unsold.

VINTAGE, BANDANNA

ヴィンテージ、バンダナ

product : bandana
made in : U.S.A.

material : cotton cotton × polyester

デニムやチノパンのヒップポケットから
約10㎜ほどのぞかせる

Put it in the hip pocket of denims or chinos
and show it about 10㎜.

私がお洒落に目覚めた頃には、バンダナをパンツのバックポケットに
入れているジーンズショップやセレクトショップの先達がたくさんいまし
た。見た目がお洒落という以外には特に大きな意味合いはなく、みん
なが思い思いのスタイルでポケットに入れていたと思います。時代を
遡ってみると、カウボーイの実用品として、またアメリカでは同性愛の
男性であることを示すものとして。様々な文化的背景を含んで使われ
てきたようですが、私としては当時憧れたショップスタッフの方たちと
同様に、今も実用性から離れたファッション感覚で愛用しています。
例えば、ジャケットの胸ポケットに挿すチーフとちょうど同じ要領で、
その日の洋服の色合わせに応じてバンダナの色を選んでいます。この
感覚は、クラシック畑の人間である私ならではかもしれません。

When I came to be interested in clothes, many shop staff put a
bandanna in their hip pockets at jeans shops and multi-brand
shops. It didn't mean anything special other than trying to look
cool, and I think everyone did so in their own style. Looking back
the history of bandannas, they were actually used for practical
reasons by cowboys, and there was a time when they were used
as indications of being homosexual men in the United States.
Bandannas have been used with various cultural backgrounds, but
I use them only to make my style just like the shop staff I admired
at the time. For example, I choose a bandana color according to the
color of the clothes of the day, just like the pocket square that I put
in the chest pocket of my jacket. This sense may be unique to men
like me who engage in classic clothes field.

VINTAGE, COLLAR PIN
ヴィンテージ、カラーピン

product : collar pin

made in : upper & middle upper/U.S.A.
middle lower & lower/Japan

material : upper & middle upper/gold plated×metal
middle lower/gold plated×silver 925   lower/silver 925

クラシックを愛する者として
これくらいは使いこなしたい

Classic style lovers should master this at least.

私がカラーピンを初めて買ったのは20年ほど前。新品が流通していなかったため、ヴィンテージを探して手に入れました(写真中上)。しかし、当時のシャツはワイドスプレッドカラーが主流だったため、襟をピンで刺すことができず……。ボタンダウンシャツなどにしか使えずに悲しい思いをした記憶があります。そもそもカラーピンは、1930〜60年代の映画でフレッド・アステアなどがしばしば着用していたアイテム。小さく結んだノットが美しく立ち上がるネクタイのエレガントな雰囲気はいつ見ても美しく、私を魅了してやみません。なお、ストライプのタイなどスポーティな雰囲気のアイテムに合わせても良いのですが、私が特に好きなのが大柄のプリントタイを用いたクラシックなスーツスタイル。Vゾーンからエレガントなオーラが香り立ちます。

I bought a color pin for the first time about 20 years ago. At that time, there were not much new products in market, so I searched for a vintage and got it (upper in the photo). However, wide spread collars were the mainstream for shirts at that time, so I didn't have many shirts that I could stab collars with the pin... I remember feeling sad because it could only be used for button-down shirts. The color pin is an item that was worn by Fred Astaire and many other actors in movies from the 30s to the 60s. The elegant look of the tie, where a small knot stands up beautifully, is always beautiful and fascinates me. You can match it with items with a sporty style such as striped ties, but I especially like the classic suit style with a large print tie. An elegant aura scents from the chest.

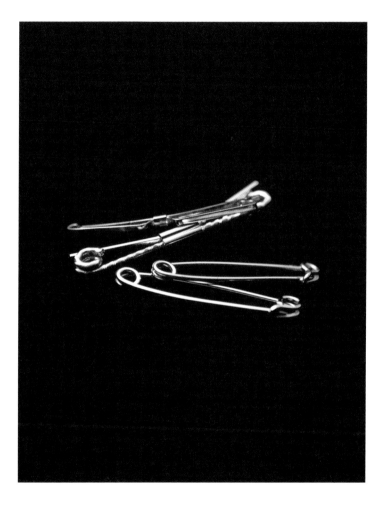

WALLET COMME DES GARÇONS
ZIP WALLET

ウォレット・コム・デ・ギャルソン、ジップウォレット

product : wallet   made in Spain

material : calf leather

シンプルで飾らないデザインが
自分史上最高に使える財布

The best wallet I have ever had is
a simple and undecorated design.

このアイテムの魅力を紹介するためには、少し私の財布遍歴を振り返る必要があります。ドレスクロージングに従事するようになり、まず憧れたのはマネークリップでした。その後、札入れとコインケースを分けて持つようになり、エキゾチックレザーの長財布とコインケースを持っていた時期も。ただ、そんな風に背伸びをしている自分に違和感を持ち、シンプルな財布を探すようになりました。若い頃よりも様々な服を着る今の自分にとって何が最適なのかと考えていた時に出会ったのが、この財布です。ブラックカーフとゴールドジップで内装もブラックという極めてシンプルな作りが、今の自分にとてもフィットしています。とにかく、無駄がなく使いやすい。コインがやや取り出しにくい点以外は、ほぼパーフェクトだと思える素晴らしい財布です。

To introduce the charm of this item, I need to explain a bit on my wallet history. When I started my career in dress clothing, I longed for a money clip. Then, I had a billfold and a coin case separately. There was even a period when I had an exotic leather billfold and a coin case. However, I came to feel uncomfortable with myself trying to look mature like that, and I began to search for a simple wallet. I was wondering what was best for me who wears more various types of clothes than before, and I finally met this wallet. The extremely simple construction with black calf body, gold zip, and black interior seems to fit me well. It's simple and easy to use with good storage capacity of bills, coins, and cards. It's a great wallet that seems almost perfect except that it's a bit difficult to take out coins.

n⁰ 042

—

n⁰ 047

Bag

バッグは男性が身に着けられる
最大面積のアクセサリーです

Bags are the largest accessary
that a man can wear.

COACH,
1980S DRAWSTRING BAG
コーチ、1980年代製 巾着バッグ

product : drawstring bag made in U.S.A.

material : cowhide leather

甘さと強さが見事に調和した
グローブレザー製の巾着バッグ

A drawstring bag made of glove leather
that perfectly harmonizes sweetness and strength.

オールドコーチの定番といえるバケツ型バッグは以前から所有していた
のですが、その風合いの良さを気に入って、ほかのモデルも欲しくな
りました。そして、数年かけて探して出会ったのが、この1980年代に
製造された巾着バッグです。ブランドの代名詞であるグローブレザー
を使用した希少なアイテム。ヴィンテージショップの奥の方に無造作に
陳列されていましたが、キラリと光る存在感を放っていました。フォル
ムは女性的でありながら、革の持つ独特の質感や金具の雰囲気が武
骨なので、男性が持っても十分に成立します。メンズバッグブランド
ではあまり見られない柔らかい印象と、堅牢な作りとを両立し、甘さ
と強さのバランスが見事です。必要最小限の手荷物が入る絶妙なサイ
ズ感も秀逸。ちょっとした外出時に重宝する、相棒的な存在です。

I have owned a bucket-shaped bag, which is said to be a classic of
old COACH. I like its good texture and wanted other models as well.
So, I spent several years searching for and came across this
drawstring bag manufactured in the 80s. It is a rare item made of
glove leather, which is said to be synonymous with the brand. It was
displayed casually in the back of the vintage shop, but I felt a
brilliant presence from it. Although the form is feminine, the
unique texture of the leather and the metal fittings are rugged,
which is why it's a good bag for as well. It has a soft impression that
is not often seen in men's bags, as well as a durable construction,
and such balance between sweetness and strength is wonderful. The
exquisite size that can hold the minimum required baggage is also
excellent. It is a handy companion when I go out for a while.

CROOTS, BRIEFCASE
クルーツ、ブリーフケース

product : briefcase   made in England

material : bridle leather

ひらめきをカタチにした 現代における究極の英国バッグ
The ultimate British bag in the modern era shaped from inspiration.

このブランドの展示会で、バッグとして実用に耐えうる限界まで薄くすいたブライドルレザーを見た瞬間に、「この革を使って、軽い英国バッグを作れないだろうか」というインスピレーションが浮かびました。アイデアと熱意をブランド側に伝え、英国バッグやブライドルレザーバッグの既成概念を覆そうというコンセプトで完全別注したのが、このブリーフケースです。イギリスのバッグブランドとしては珍しく、革をレーザーカットしているため裁断面がこの上なく美しい仕上がりに。さらに、1枚の革を折り畳んで作られているので、表情も限りなくシンプル。少し変わったモダンな留め金具は、イギリスというよりもむしろフランスっぽい雰囲気です。自分が気に入って別注したアイテムゆえに、思い入れもひとしお。現代における究極の英国バッグだと自負しています。

At an exhibition of this brand, I saw bridle leather that is thinned to the limit to be used as a bag. At the moment, an inspiration came to me, "Maybe I can make a light British bag using this leather." I enthusiastically told the brand about my idea of making a bespoke bag with a concept to overturn the preconceived notions of British bags and bridle leather bags. Unusual for a British bag brand, the leather is laser-cut for a beautiful finish. Furthermore, because it is made by folding a piece of leather, it looks infinitely simple. Slightly unique modern latch looks more French than British. Because it is customized, it is special for me. I take pride in this bag being the ultimate British bag of our time.

n.º 044

HELEN KAMINSKI,
RAFFIA TOTE BAG

ヘレンカミンスキー、ラフィアトートバッグ

product : tote bag   made in : Sri Lanka

material : raffia × leather

人の手の温もりを感じられる
夏専用バッグ

A summer bag that allows you
to feel the warmth of handmade.

伝統工芸品のような手の温かみを感じられるモノには、人を惹きつけ
る不思議な魅力があります。ヘレンカミンスキーの製品も然り。日本
では、コンパクトに畳めるカジュアルな雰囲気のラフィア製ハットで有
名なブランドですが、時間をかけて職人の手で編み上げられたラフィ
アブレードは、しなやかでありながら耐久性にも優れ、使い込むほど
に光沢が増していくのが特徴です。このトートバッグにも、ハットと同
じくマダガスカル島の良質なラフィアが使用されており、「これこそが
探し求めていた夏用バッグだ」と出会った瞬間に直感しました。究極
的にシンプルなデザインゆえ、夏の軽やかな装いに幅広く合わせるこ
とが可能。かつ、この上なくエレガントで洒落て見えるのは、人の手
によって丹精込めて作られたモノであることの証といえます。

Things that you can feel the warmth of hands like traditional
crafts have a subtle charm that attracts people. So are Helen
Kaminski's products. In Japan, the brand is famous for its casual
raffia hats that can be folded compactly. The raffia blades, woven
by craftsmen over time, are supple yet durable, and the more you
use them, the glossier they become. Same as hats, this is a tote bag
made of high-quality raffia from Madagascar, and I instantly felt,
"This is the summer bag I was looking for", when I first met it. Its
ultimately simple design makes it possible to match a wide range
of casual summer outfits. Moreover, the fact that it looks extremely
elegant and stylish is the proof that it was made with great care by
craftsmen's hands.

HERVÉ CHAPELIER,
DAY PACK 879NM

エルベシャプリエ、デイパック 879NM

product : day pack   made in France

material : nylon

ドレススタイルに合う
唯一無二のリュックサック

The one and only rucksack
that suits your dressy style.

エルベシャプリエといえば、大人のリュックサックの代名詞的ブランド。現在に至るまで形や素材、そして生産背景を含めて様々なバリエーションが展開されてきました。その中で個人的なNo.1は、いまや絶版となったこのフランス製です。その理由は、サイズがコンパクトであること。ドレススタイルをメインに着る私にとっては、これくらい華奢なサイズ感がもっともフィットします。モノを入れると下部に荷重がかかるため、実際の大きさよりもさらに華奢に見えるのがお気に入りです。また、薄くて軽いナイロンには上品な光沢があるため、革靴に革鞄がセオリーとされるドレススタイルに合わせるのもアリだと思わせてくれます。大人としてはジャケットやカジュアルなスーツに合わせる際には、片側のストラップだけ肩掛けして"ハズし"が"ハズレ"にならないよう気をつけています。

Hervé Chapelier is a synonymous brand with rucksacks for adults. Until now, it has developed a various types of rucksack with different shapes, materials, and production backgrounds. But the ones made in France, which are not produced anymore, are the best for me. The reason is that it is compact. For me, who mainly wear dressy outfits, this delicate size fits the best. I like that it looks even more delicate than the actual size when you put things in it and they push down the bottom of the bag. In addition, thin and light nylon has an elegant luster, which makes me think that this bag looks good even with dressy styles. When matching with a jacket or casual suit, I hang only one strap on my shoulder so that I do not spoil the elegant style.

HUNTING WORLD, SHOULDER BAG
ハンティング・ワールド、ショルダーバッグ

product : shoulder bag made in Italy

material : canvas

若い頃には気づくことが できなかった魅力を発見

Discovering the charms
that I couldn't notice when I was young.

私が若い頃は、ハンティング・ワールドに対してなんとなくおじさん臭くて垢抜けないイメージを持っていました。1990年代にバチュークロスのシリーズが大流行したこともあり、私の父親世代がこぞって持っていたからです。しかし、モノととことん向き合う仕事に携わるようになってからは、素材や縫製、金具などのパーツまでこだわり抜いたその作りの良さに、感動すら覚えるようになりました。ヘビーキャンバスとゴールドの金具という組み合わせが珍しいこのモデルは、私自身が世に言う"おじさん"の年齢になった数年前に購入したもの。歳を重ねたおかげで自然とフィットするようになったわけですが、このバッグの名誉を守るためにも、若者から「アイツが持っているバッグ、おじさん臭い」と絶対に思われないようにしなければ、と心に誓っています。

To be honest, when I was young, my image of Hunting World is "middle-aged men" and "unrefined". This was because many people in my father's generation owned its bags when the Battue Cloth series became very popular in the 90s. However, since I became involved in the work of fashion designs and productions thoroughly, I was impressed and even moved by the quality of materials, sewing, and metal fittings of the brand. This model, which is a rare combination of heavy canvas and gold metal fittings, was the one I purchased a few years ago when I became so-called "middle-aged" man. Thanks to my age, it naturally fits me. In order to protect the honor of this bag, I swear to my heart that I have to make sure that young people never think that "That bag he has looks like an old man's bag".

RALPH LAUREN,
1990S SAFARI LINE OVERNIGHTER BAG
ラルフ ローレン、1990年代製 サファリライン オーバーナイターバッグ

product : overnighter bag

made in Korea

material : canvas × leather

実用性を超越する魅力を備えた
重量級の相棒

A heavyweight companion with a charm
that transcends practicality.

クラシックな装いをするうえで欠かせない"サファリスタイル"に合う雰囲気のバッグを、ずっと探していました。そんな折、何かの雑誌でこのバッグを見つけ、自分が思い描いていたイメージ通りのルックスにひと目惚れ。ただし、業界人の中でも名コレクションと言われる、1992年発表のサファリラインの希少なモデルということもあり、実際に手に入れるまでには数年を要しました。ヴィンテージショップでついに出会えた瞬間の感動は半端ではなかったのですが、その重量も衝撃的でした。荷物を入れると、筋トレかと思うほどの重さになってしまい、使い勝手が良いとは決していえません。しかし、真鍮の金具や硬いキャンバス、ブリティッシュの空気感とラギッドなアメリカの雰囲気が同居したデザインには、その不便さを補って余りある魅力が溢れているのです。

I had always looked for a bag that matches "safari style", which is one of indispensable classic looks. I found this bag in a magazine and fell in love at first sight with the look that I had imagined. However, it took several years to actually own it because it is a rare model from the safari line in 1992, which is a famous collection among fashion lovers. I was shocked and moved when I finally found it at a vintage shop, but its weight was also shocking. If you put some stuff in it, it gets as heavy as you are doing some weight training, so it's never easy to use. However, the design, which involves brass fittings, hard canvas, the British character and rugged American vibes, is worth more than compensating for its weight.

nº 048
—
nº 078

Clothing (European)

イギリス、フランス、イタリア
みんな違って、みんな良い

England, France, Italy
They are all different and all wonderful.

AGNÈS B.,
STRIPED T-SHIRT

アニエスベー、Tシャツ

product : t-shirt ········· made in Japan ·····························

material : cotton ···

若かりし日に心震わせた
モノとコトにいまだに惹かれる

Still fascinated by the items and things
that shook my heart when young.

高校時代、アルバイト代を握り締めてドキドキしながらアニエスベーの
お店へ足を運びました。そして、ボーダーのTシャツと黒のコットンパ
ンツを購入。通い慣れたヴィンテージショップではなく、生まれて初
めてブランドのショップで買い物できたことで気分が高揚し、自分が
ちょっぴり大人になった気分に。当時の私としては、入店を躊躇する
ほど憧れの存在であり、またファッションの原体験のひとつだったよう
に思います。あれから20年以上が経ち、今の私にとってこのブランド
のボーダーカットソーは、日常着の定番といえる等身大のアイテムとな
りました。ちなみに、ラガーシャツから着想を得たとされるこのコット
ン天竺編みの硬いボーダーカットソーにいまだに強く惹かれてしまうの
は、私が中高時代にラガーマンだったからなのかもしれません。

When I was a high school student, I went to a shop of agnès b.,
nervously holding my money that I had earned for a part-time job.
I bought a striped T-shirt and black cotton pants. By shopping at
a brand shop for the first time in my life, rather than the vintage
shops I had always been to, I felt very uplifted and a little grown-
up. At that time, I admired the brand so much that I even hesitated
to enter the store.It was one of my first fashion-related experiences.
About 20 years have passed since then, and for me now, the striped
T-shirts of this brand have become life-sized items that are staples of
my everyday wear. In addition, maybe because I played rugby in my
junior high and high school, I am still strongly fascinated by these
stiff striped T-shirts of cotton plain knitting, which are said to have
been inspired by rugby shirts.

ALFONSO SIRICA, LINEN SUIT

アルフォンソ シリカ、リネンスーツ

product : suit ------------------------------- made in Italy ----------------------------------

material : linen ---

いつかナポリの海岸を
歩きたいと思わせるリネンスーツ

Someday I want to walk along the coast of Naples
in this linen suit.

ナポリを代表するサルトの中で、ダルクオーレはどちらかというとクラシックな温もりがある印象。一方、アルフォンソ シリカは既製品として美しく成立する安定感があり、まだド直球なハンドメイドのナポリ服という雰囲気も感じさせます。それは、精緻な型紙を製作するためにナポリサルトとしては極めて稀なCADと呼ばれる設計システムを導入しつつ、一針一針丁寧にハンドで縫い上げていくという、一見相反するようにも思われるモノ作りの工程を踏んでいるからにほかなりません。このスーツは、イギリスのスペンス・ブライソン社のリネン100%の生地を使用。程良いゆとりを持たせたシルエットで、風にそよぐ感じが美しい。あえて夏に深いダークブラウンを着ることで優雅な空気感を演出できます。これを着て、いつかナポリの海岸を歩きたいですね。

Among the representative sartoria in Naples, Dalcuore has rather classic warmth. On the other hand, Alfonso Sirica has stability to manufacture beautiful ready-made clothes. At the same time, its clothes make you feel the pure vibes of handmade clothes in Naples. In its manufacturing process, each stitch is carefully sewn by hand just like other sartoria in Naples, but it also utilizes a computer design system called CAD in order to produce a precise pattern, which is extremely rare for Neapolitan sartoria. This suit is made from 100% Spence Bryson linen. The silhouette has a moderate amount of space, and it beautifully sways in the wind. By wearing this deep dark brown suit in summer, it creates elegant vibes. I want to walk along the coast of Naples in this suit someday.

n⁰ 050

ALFREDO RIFUGIO,
SUEDE JACKET

アルフレッド・リフージオ、スエードジャケット

product : jacket　　　　　　　　　　　made in　Italy

material : goat suede

レザーの既製服において
最高到達点といえる存在

The ultimate ready-made leather jacket.

このジャケットの原型は、茶系のゴートスエード素材で4つボタンのダ
ブルブレストジャケット型。それをブラックスエードとゴールドメタルボ
タンで特別な仕様にしてもらいました。先方より「ブラックスエードは
色落ちの懸念があるのでやめた方が良いのでは?」と止められました
が、「洋服屋である私個人が着用する分にはまったく問題なし!」と答
えたのを覚えています。極限まで薄く鞣したきめ細やかなゴートスエ
ードは、上質であることがひと目でわかります。さらにテーラードのア
イテムに見られるような立体的なパターンで仕立てられているため、そ
の着心地はもはや着ていることを忘れてしまうほど快適。私がこれま
で着てきたレザージャケットの中でもっともラグジュアリーであり、また
レザーの既製服において最高到達点のひとつといえます。

The prototype of this jacket is a brown goat suede double-breasted
jacket with 4 buttons. I had it made into a special specification with
black suede and gold metal buttons. They tried to stop me, saying,
"It would be better to avoid black suede because there is a concern
about discoloration." I remember answering, "I, as a clothier, will
personally wear it, so there is no problem at all!" At a glance, you
can see that the fine goat suede, which is tanned as thin as possible,
is of high quality. In addition, it is tailored with a three-dimensional
pattern just like tailored items, and it is so comfortable to wear that
I sometimes forget that I am wearing it. Alfredo Rifugio is one of
the most luxurious leather jackets I've ever worn and one of the best
ready-made leather garments.

nº 051

AQUASCUTUM,
TRENCH COAT
アクアスキュータム、トレンチコート

product : coat   made in Canada

material : cotton

ようやく出会えた
理想的なサイジングのトレンチコート

The trench coat of ideal size
that I finally met.

アクアスキュータムとバーバリーといえば、トレンチコートの二大ブランド。私は以前からどちらのブランドのトレンチも所有していましたが、いずれもイギリス製のものは肩がポッコリと膨らんでおり、まるで"昭和のサラリーマン"のように見えてしまい、とても満足のいくものではありませんでした。その後、納得のいくサイズやフォルムのものに買い換えようとしていたタイミングで出会ったのが、このカナダ製のアクアスキュータムです。イギリス製のものと同じ38サイズ表記ですが、肩がストンと美しく落ちる理想的なサイズバランス。また、現行モデルとは異なり、袖や着丈の先端までライニングが行き届いていて、細部までしっかりと作り込まれていることがわかります。洋服を扱う立場にある私としては、資料性も高く非常に価値のある一着なのです。

Aquascutum and Burberry are two major brands of trench coats. I had owned trench coats of both brands, but the ones made in England have bulging shoulders and look like "Japanese office workers in the Showa era", so I was not very satisfied with them. When I wanted to buy a new one with a size and shape that I like, I came across this Aquascutum's trench coat made in Canada. The size 38 notation is the same as the one made in England, but this one had an ideal size with natural shoulders. Also, unlike the current model, you can see that the lining is perfect to the sleeves and the tip of the length, and the details are well thought-out. For me as a fashion director, it is also a very valuable piece of clothing as a reference material.

AVINO LABORATORIO NAPOLETANO, CUSTOM-MADE SHIRT

アヴィーノ・ラボラトリオ・ナポレターノ、オーダーメイドシャツ

product : shirt   made in Italy

material : cotton

手縫いのシャツの素晴らしい着心地と力強い佇まいとの邂逅

Hand-sewn shirt combining
a wonderful comfort and a strong shape.

「メンズのドレスシャツはどこの国が一番か」という問いへの見解は人それぞれ。イギリス、フランス、アメリカ、イタリア等々が挙げられるはずですが、着心地の良いシャツという観点からいえば、個人的にはイタリアが群を抜いていると思います。その理由は、いまや他国ではほぼ途絶えてしまった手縫いの技術を職人が受け継いでいく文化そのものが、イタリアには根強く残っているから。アヴィーノ・ラボラトリオ・ナポレターノのシャツは、そんなイタリアで"仕立ての街"として知られるナポリの伝統的な手法で作られています。襟型やボディから受ける印象はすこぶる男性的。だからこそ、クラシックな洋服を男らしく見せてくれます。オーナーが、私の愛してやまないナポリのスーツ職人ルイジ・ダルクオーレ氏に師事していたことも納得です。

Each person has their own views on the question, "Which country makes the best dress shirts for men?" The United Kingdom, France, the United States, Italy, etc. should be mentioned, but from the perspective of the most comfortable shirts, I personally think that Italy is by far the best. The reason for that is its culture itself, in which craftsmen inherit hand-sewn techniques that are almost non-existent in other countries. Avino Laboratorio Napoletano shirts are made in the traditional way of Naples, known as the "city of tailoring" in Italy. The impression received from the collar and body is very masculine, which is why it makes classic clothes look masculine. This brand makes wonderful shirts, and it's no surprise to hear that Mr. Francesco Alvino learned tailoring under Luigi Dalcuore, a Neapolitan tailor I love.

nº 053

BARBOUR,
CLASSIC BEDALE
バブアー、クラシック ビデイル

product : jacket   made in England

material : cotton

紆余曲折あってようやく手に入れた
自分なりのエレガンス考

My own thoughts on elegance that entered my head
after twists and turns.

バブアーのクラシック ビデイルを初めて知ったのは20歳くらいの時。
アメカジ一辺倒を卒業して、大人っぽい服に興味を持ったタイミング
でした。当時すでに流行っていて、ブルージーンズにトリッカーズのカ
ントリーブーツを合わせた装いをよく目にしたものです。ただ、いつか
は手に入れるべきアイテムだとは思いつつ、周りと同じような着こなし
はしたくなく、一度は保留に……。数年後に手にしてからは、フレン
チっぽくモノトーンのカントリースタイルに合わせていました。しかし、
独特なにおいを女性から指摘され、「これは自分の生活様式で着る服
ではない」と思い早々に手放してしまいました。現在所有しているのは、
のちに展開されたドライワックスのもの。人に礼を失したり不快な思い
をさせたりする服をまとうことは、エレガントとはいえませんから。

I first learned about Barbour's Classic Bedale when I was about
20 years old. It was the time when I had gone through American
casual fashion and became interested in more grown-up looking
clothes. Bedale was already popular at the time, and I often saw
people wearing them with blue jeans and Tricker's country boots.
Although I thought it's an item I should get someday, I did not want
to wear it in the same way as others around me did. So I did not
buy it soon. I bought it after a few years later, and I matched it in
a French-ish monotone country style. However, when I was in my
twenties, a woman pointed out its distinct odor of waxed fabric, and
I quickly let it go, thinking, "This is not the clothes I should wear
in my lifestyle." I currently own a Drywax model that was released
later, because I think that wearing clothes that make people feel
unpleasant is not elegant.

BERNARD ZINS,
TROUSERS

ベルナール ザンス、トラウザーズ

product : trousers　　　　made in　Portugal

material : wool

確固たる信念のもと生み出される
無二のドレスパンツ

Unrivaled dress pants that are created
with a firm philosophy.

ベルナール ザンスを初めて購入したのは20年ほど前。ハイバックのノープリーツ仕様で裾幅20 〜 21cmのストレートシルエットでした。イタリアモノ全盛期において、フレンチの薫りが漂うこのテイストは非常に新鮮でした。そして、15年前に購入したモデルにも、ここ2、3年ほどで新調した写真の2本にも、ブランドの揺るぎない個性が宿っています。以前、ブランドの現社長であるフランク・ザンス氏から、「何年もの間、まったく同じ生地を用意しているのは、自分の"これだ"という強い信念を貫いているからだ」と聞いたことがあります。確固たる哲学を持ってパンツを作り続ける姿勢に感銘を受けました。1本のパンツを長く追求するザンス氏と、良いモノを長く愛用する私に共通点を見出せたことが、なによりうれしかったですね。

I first bought Bernard Zins trousers about 20 years ago. They were with straight cut, a high back, no pleats, and a hem width of 20-21 cm. In the heyday of Italian clothes in Japan, this style with French vibes was very fresh to me. Both the model I bought 15 years ago and the two new models that I bought in the last 3 years have the brand's unwavering characteristics. Frank Zins, the current president of the brand once said, "We have used the same fabrics for years because we have a strong belief that they are the best." I was impressed with his attitude of continuing to make quality trousers with a firm philosophy. Above all, I was happy to find the commonality between Mr. Zins, who loves each pair of trousers for a long time, and me, who loves quality items for a long time.

BURBERRY, 1990S HARRINGTON JACKET
バーバリー、1990年代製 ハリントンジャケット

product : jacket　　　　　　　　made in England

material : cotton × polyurethane

"これ見よがし"が"さり気なさ"へと 変化する瞬間を大切に

Treasure the moment
when "showy" changes to "modestly stylish".

バーバリーのハリントンジャケットは、古着店の壁に掛かっているのを見た瞬間にひと目惚れし、試着したらジャストサイズだったので即購入。ラグランスリーブのモデルはたまに見かけますが、セットインスリーブのものはレアで、私も初めて見ました。襟裏や袖裏のバーバリーチェックに「襟を立てたり、袖を捲ったりして着てください」といわれているようで、ブランドならではの主張が感じられるのも良いですね。クラシックな洋服は主張がなく中庸なものがほとんどですが、このアイテムには"これ見よがし"な感じがあります。ただ、その感じも何十年という時を経ることで"あざとさ"が不思議と薄れていくもの。そして、そのあざとさが限りなくゼロに近づいて上手く料理できたタイミングこそ、"これ見よがし"が"さり気ないお洒落"へと変わる瞬間なのです。

I fell in love with Burberry's Harrington jacket the moment I saw it hanging on the wall of a vintage shop. I tried it on, and it was just the right size for me, so I bought it. I sometimes find its raglan sleeve model, but its set-in sleeve model is rare, and actually it was my first time to see it. The Burberry checks on the back of the collar and sleeves seem to say, "Turn up your collar" or "Roll up your sleeves", and I like such presence. Most of the classic clothes are unassuming and moderate, but this item has a kind of showy feel. However, that feeling also mysteriously fades over the course of decades. And, the timing when such feeling approaches zero and you style it well is the moment when "showy" changes to "modestly stylish".

CINQUANTA,
B-3 1ST MODEL
チンクワンタ、B-3 ファーストモデル

product : jacket   made in Italy

material : shearling leather × horsehide leather

こだわりを詰め込んだB-3は
西口式の着こなしで

The B-3, made with full commitment,
is styled in Nishiguchi way.

初期のディテールを踏襲したこのB-3は、古い資料なども参考にしながらチンクワンタに細部まで徹底的に作り込んでもらった別注品。本物のアメリカ軍のB-3は重く、革が分厚く非常にラギッドなアウターなのに対し、こちらは革の厚さを調整することで柔らかく、それでいて本格的なディテールはしっかりと残してあるため、現代的に着るにはちょうど良い雰囲気に仕上がっています。柔らかく上質なムートンは、機能的な服として生まれたミリタリーウェアの本来の目的である保温性を十分に確保しながらも上品。そんな私のこだわりが詰まったB-3は、あえてプレッピーテイストのブラウンスーツと組み合わせることによって、小気味良く着こなしています。誰もやっていないような着方で服のポテンシャルを引き出すことも、私たち洋服屋の使命ですから。

This B-3, with the details of its early model, is a bespoke jacket by Cinquanta, based on our requests in details that we referred from old materials. The real U.S. Army B-3 is too heavy and looks rugged, because it's made of thick leather. On the other hand, this updated B-3, with full-fledged details, is softer thanks to thinner leather, making it more wearable and comfortable. The soft, high-quality mouton looks elegant, while ensuring sufficient heat retention, which is the original purpose of military wear born as functional clothes. I style my bespoke B-3 with my brown suit tailored in a preppy taste, for a smart look. It is our mission, as clothiers, to bring out the potential of clothes, by styling them in the way no one else do.

CINQUANTA,
HORSEHIDE RIDER'S JACKET

チンクワンタ、ホースハイド ライダーズジャケット

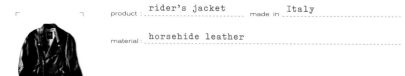

product : rider's jacket   made in   Italy

material : horsehide leather

硬派なのに気構えることなく
幅広く着こなせるのが魅力

A manly jacket that you can wear in various styles
without thinking too much.

ライダーズというとその名の如くバイカーのためのジャケットと考える方
も多いかもしれません。しかしチンクワンタが手がけたアイテムは、そ
の概念に収まらない魅力を持っています。街着としても成立する薄くて
堅牢なホースハイド製で、細すぎず太すぎない立体的なシルエットが
特徴。本来のライダーズらしくデニムで男らしく合わせても、テーラー
ドジャケット感覚でウールパンツにタイドアップして上品に仕上げても
サマになります。また、イタリアらしく洗練された雰囲気を備えている
点も良い。ラギッドな雰囲気を全面に押し出した専業ブランドのもの
とは異なり、気構えずに着ることができます。一方で、色気のあるアイ
テムが多いイタリアブランドの中において、比較的に硬派な印象を感
じられる点も、チンクワンタの素晴らしい個性です。

Many people may think that rider's jackets are for bikers, as the
name suggests. However, this item created by Cinquanta has
charms that do not fit into that concept. Made of thin and durable
horsehide that can be used as street wear, it has a three-dimensional
silhouette that is neither too slim nor too big. That's why, you look
great, even if you match it with denim like people do, or if you wear
it with a tie and wool pants like a tailored jacket. It is also nice that
this jacket has sophisticated vibes that are unique to Italian brands.
You can wear it without thinking too much, unlike the products
of specialized brands that extrude rugged vibes all over. On the
other hand, among the Italian brands, which have many items with
amorous images, you can feel a relatively rigid image, which is
also a wonderful charm of Cinquanta.

CRUCIANI,
MERINO WOOL HIGH GAUGE KNIT

クルチアーニ、メリノウール ハイゲージニット

product : knit pullover .... made in Italy ....

material : wool ....

イタリア服のモダンな魅力を
体感できる最高品質のニット

The highest quality knit that allows you to experience
the modern charm of Italian clothing.

今から20年くらい前までは、メリノのハイゲージニットといえばジョンスメドレー一択。そんな中、シンプルながら洗練されたデザインと最高品質の素材を兼ね備えたクルチアーニが登場し、業界内で大きな話題を呼びました。当時、私たち華奢な日本人は、着丈が長くゆったりとしたジョンスメドレーをブラウジングしてなんとか着ていましたが、クルチアーニは着丈がやや短めの設定。タックアウトしても野暮ったく見えない、スッキリとしたシルエットで着こなすことができたのです。ショップスタッフをはじめ、クラシック好きの皆が入荷のたびに買い漁っていましたね。当時はジョンスメドレーと同じ価格帯だったことも若かりし日の自分にはありがたい存在でした。無駄がなくシンプルで高品質なイタリアのニットといえば、今もやっぱりこのブランドです。

Until about 20 years ago, John Smedley seemed the only choice for merino wool high-gauge knitwear in Japan. So when we first knew Cruciani, which combines a simple yet sophisticated design with the highest quality materials, it instantly become a hot topic in the industry. At that time, short and slim Japanese men put the hem of the long and loose John Smedley into pants. On the other hand, Cruciani had slightly shorter lengths, so even if I kept its hem out of my pants, I was able to dress in a neat silhouette that looked stylish. Everyone who loves classic styles, including shop staff, bought Cruciani every time they arrived. Unlike today, the price range was around the same as John Smedley at that time. When it comes to lean, simple and high quality Italian knitwear, Cruciani is the best for me.

131

DALCUORE,
BESPOKE 4B DOUBLE BREASTED SUIT
ダルクオーレ、フルオーダー 4B ダブルブレストスーツ

product : suit   made in Italy

material : wool

初めてフルオーダーで仕立てた
思い出深いスーツ

A memorable suit tailored
by full order for the first time.

仮縫い込みのフルオーダーを経験したことのなかった私が、30代後半
で初めてのオーダー先として選んだのがダルクオーレです。型紙を持
たず、顧客の要望に合わせて作り上げていくこのブランドのスタイル
は、まさにナポリサルトの真骨頂。顧客のリクエストに対してアグレッ
シブに、そしてポジティブに応えてくれます。自分たちのスタイルを崩
さない、いわゆる昔気質のサルトが多い中、ダルクオーレのようなサ
ルトは珍しい存在。その柔軟な姿勢は、自分たちの技術への絶対的
な自信の表れでしょう。私はこのスーツをあえてサルト側の意見も多分
にデザインに反映させたダルクオーレスタイルで作りました。初めての
フルオーダーで、洋服屋としてもひとりの服好きとしても素晴らしい経
験をさせてくれた彼らに対する、私なりの敬意です。

Personally I had never made a fully tailor-made suit until my late
thirties. I chose Dalcuore as my first sartoria to make my first
bespoke suit. They do not use a paper pattern, but instead their suits
are tailored exactly to clients' needs. They are aggressive and happy
to work for clients. This is the true value of Neapolitan sartoria.
While there are many so-called old-fashioned sartoria that never go
out of their own styles, sartoria like Dalcuore are rare. That flexible
attitude is a sign of absolute confidence in their technology. I
dared to make this suit in the Dalcuore style, which reflected many
opinions of the Sartoria side in the design. I wanted to show my
respect for them that made my first full-order suit and gave me a
wonderful experience, both as a clothier and as a fashion enthusiast.

DE PETRILLO, TWEED JACKET
デ・ペトリロ、ツイードジャケット

product : jacket ---------------------- made in Italy --------------------

material : wool --

伸縮性のないデッドストック生地を
ナポリ仕立てで快適に

Tailored comfortably in Naples style
from non-stretchable deadstock fabric.

趣のあるヘビーウエイトの生地によって非常に渋いオーラを放つこのジャケットは、イギリス製のデッドストック生地が気に入って個人オーダーをしたもの。どことなく年代物のアメリカ製品にも似た、良い意味で堅い表情なので、アメリカモノとの相性は抜群です。しかし、私はそれに縛られることなくイギリス、イタリア、そしてフランスと、様々な国のアイテムを自由にミックスして着るようにしています。そのくらい、このジャケットはコーディネートの可能性を秘めていると思っているからです。ただしデッドストックの生地は伸縮性がまったくなく、着心地が良いとは言いにくいのですが、さすがペトリロ。見た目の美しさだけでなく着心地にも重きを置いたナポリ仕立てのブランドゆえ、動きにくさは最小限に抑えられているのがポイントです。

The quaint heavyweight fabric gives off a very quiet aura, and it's my personal-order jacket that is made of deadstock fabric and tailored by De Petrillo. It has a solid look in a good way that is somewhat similar to vintage American products, so it goes well with American items. However, I don't do it only, instead, I freely mix and wear items from various countries such as Britain, Italy, and France. I think this jacket has the potential to make you feel the expansion of coordination possibilities. However, this deadstock fabric has no elasticity at all, so it is hard to say that it is comfortable to wear. However, thanks to De Petrillo, a Neapolitan brand that emphasizes not only aesthetics but also comfort, such difficulty to move is minimized for this jacket.

DRUMOHR,
DRUMOHR MODERN CREW NECK KNIT
ドルモア、ドルモアモダン クルーネックニット

product : crew neck knit made in Italy

material : wool

季節は春、
思わず素肌に着たくなる極上のニット

The finest knit pullover that
makes me want to wear on bare skin in spring.

新技術で開発された限りなく薄い30ゲージのメリノウールニットは、日本の気候においては特に春先に本領を発揮してくれます。そもそも私たちが生活する日本では、春夏はコットン、秋冬はウールという認識が定着しています。しかしヨーロッパ圏では通年でウールが重宝されるように、実はこのニットは春に着ると驚くほど快適なのです。肌寒い時には暖かく、暑い時には涼しく、体温を調整してくれます。さすがに高温多湿の夏に着るのは厳しいですが、それ以外の3シーズンずっと着られるのはうれしい。薄く、ナチュラルなストレッチ性があるので自然に身体に沿います。また、滑るような肌触りで思わず素肌に着たくなるほど快適。独特の光沢も魅力で、ジャケットのインナーとしてはもちろん、1枚で着ても上品に見せてくれます。

This very thin 30-gauge merino wool knit pullover that was developed with new technology, is suitable for Japanese climate, especially in early spring. In Japan, it's a common sense to wear cotton in spring and summer and wool in autumn and winter. But just as wool items come in handy all year round in Europe, this knit pullover is actually surprisingly comfortable to wear in spring. It regulates my body temperature: It makes me warm when it is cold and cool when hot. It is hard to wear it in the hot and humid summer, but I can wear it for the other three seasons. Because it's thin and has a natural stretch, it fits naturally along my body. In addition, it has a smooth feel and is so comfortable that I want to wear on my bare skin. Its unique luster is also a charm, and it looks elegant not only when I wear it as an inner of my jacket but also when I wear it only.

□ Watch & Jewelry □ Clothing(American) □ Fashion Accessory □ Bag □ Clothing(European) □ Shoes □ Others

EMPORIO ARMANI,
1990S BELTED COAT

エンポリオ アルマーニ、1990年代製 ベルテッドコート

product : coat ----------------------- made in Italy --------------------------------

material : wool --

重量級のコートに漂う
アルマーニ流のエレガンス

Armani's elegance
found in a heavyweight coat.

1980年公開のアメリカ映画『アメリカン・ジゴロ』の衣装を手がけたこ
とで一躍脚光を浴びるようになったジョルジオ・アルマーニ氏。数々
の偉業を成し遂げ、いまや"ファッション業界の生ける伝説"とまでい
われるようになった彼のブランドの洋服を、私も以前から一度は体感し
てみたいと思っていました。1990年代に作られたと推測されるこのベ
ルテッドコートは、120cmのロングレングスによる独特のシルエットと、
重量感あるウールギャバジンによって生まれるドレープが特徴的。オー
センティックなコートと比べてウエストのベルト位置が低い点も、ア
ルマーニ流の味付けといえます。クラシックを熟知しているからこそ表
現できるエレガンス。大人になりクラシックを知った今だからこそ、こ
の服の斬新さやアルマーニの偉大さに気づくことができたのです。

Giorgio Armani came into the limelight by working on the costumes
for the movie "American Gigolo" released in 1980. I have always
wanted to experience the clothes of his brand, because he has many
achievements and is now said to be the "living legend of the fashion
industry". This belted coat, which is presumed to have been made
around the 90s, features a unique silhouette with a 120cm length
and a drape created by heavy wool gabardine. The fact that the waist
belt position is set lower than those of traditional coats is Armani's
spice. He can express elegance because he is familiar with classic
styles. Now that I have grown up and learned about classic styles, I
realized the novelty of this outfit and the greatness of Armani.

no 063

FRENCH ARMY,
1950S M-47 CARGO PANTS
フランス軍、1950 年代製 M-47 カーゴパンツ

product : pants .... made in France ....

material : cotton ....

価格高騰に臆することなく
"適当に穿いてなんぼ"の軍パン

Don't be afraid of price rises;
these are just military pants to wear casually.

3〜4年前にヴィンテージショップでデットストックの状態で購入した
のが、このフランス軍のカーゴパンツ。単純に、"フランスの古いパンツ"
という認識で見た目のディテールや構造上の面白さから購入に至りま
したが、あとから深掘りしてみると実は名品だった、という私にとって
はかなり珍しい買い物です。アメリカ軍とは違い、どことなく品のある
雰囲気がこのパンツの魅力。購入時、デッドストックのものがスラック
ス畳みになってお店に並べられていた印象が残っているからか、"ドレ
ストラウザーズに似たミリタリーパンツ"という捉え方をしています。上
品で、かつデザイン的にとてもユニークなのがお気に入りです。近年
はなぜか価格が高騰してしまいましたが、所詮は軍パンなので個人
的には"適当に穿いてなんぼ"だと思っています。

I bought these French cargo pants in dead stock condition at a
vintage shop 3-4 years ago. I bought them simply because I liked
the details and the interesting structure. I only thought they are
"old French pants", but later I found that they are actually called a
masterpiece. This is quite a rare case for me how I purchase clothes.
Unlike the US military pants, the charm of them is that they have
somewhat elegant vibes. Maybe because these dead stock pants were
folded like slacks in the store, I consider them of "military pants
similar to dress trousers". I like that they have elegant vibes and
are very unique in design. In recent years, their prices have risen a
lot for some reasons, but after all, they are just military pants. So I
personally think they are something to wear casually.

nº 064

GIANFRANCO BOMMEZZADRI, CASHMERE BLAZER

ジャンフランコ ボメザドリ、カシミア製ブレザー

product : jacket　made in Italy

material : cashmere

温故知新によって生まれた ラグジュアリーを極めたブレザー

A luxurious blazer
created by studying an item in the past.

1980年代後半のブレザーブームの時、バロールというブランドが、異なるデザインのボタンを使用したクレイジーボタン仕様のブレザーを展開していました。それをデザインソースに現代的にアップデートさせたのが、このカシミアブレザーです。「数量限定で良いから、ラグジュアリーなカシミアで作りたい」とブランドにリクエストしたもので、コート用とされる目付500gほどの肉厚な生地を使用。意匠の異なるボタンは、ブランドの工場にあった様々なメタルボタンを寄せ集めました。服飾史へのオマージュとラグジュアリーへのこだわり、そして遊び心溢れる偶然が生んだ究極の一着です。チノパンや軍パンを合わせると生地とのコントラストがつきすぎるので、仕立ての良いグレーウールパンツや少しラギッドにヴィンテージデニムを合わせています。

During the blazer boom in the late 80s in Japan, a brand named VALOR produced unique blazers with various buttons. Based on this VALOR blazer as a design source, we updated it modernly, which resulted in this cashmere blazer. I requested the brand, "We want you to make it with luxurious cashmere, even if the quantity would be limited." The fabric used is a thick cashmere with a weight of about 500g/m, which is normally used to make coats. Buttons with different designs are a collection of various metal buttons found in the factory of the brand Produced by chance, this is the ultimate blazer that is a homage to the history of clothing, embodying my commitment to luxury fashion and joy. When you matched chinos of military pants with this jacket, the contrast with the fabric would be too strong, so I enjoy pairing with well-tailored grey wool trousers with solid creases or with slightly rugged vintage jeans.

GRENFELL,
CAPE

グレンフェル、ケープ

product : cape   made in England

material : cotton

そこはかとない品の良さを感じられる
"男の雨合羽"

"Men's raincoat" that you can feel
a touch of its refined quality.

店に仕入れても絶対に売れないとわかっていながら、自分が着たい一
心でバイイングしてしまうモノが稀にあります（笑）。このケープはその
代表格。ブランドの展示会で見た瞬間に惚れ込んでしまい、直感的
に「絶対に自分のモノにしたい！」と思ってしまいました。クラシック
なデザインで比較的ミリタリー要素が強いアイテムですが、リアルなミ
リタリーウェアにはない優雅さが感じられます。これこそが、1923年
の創業以来頑なにイギリス国内でモノ作りを続けてきたグレンフェル
らしさ。ゆったりとしたケープの特性をよく捉えた、フリーサイズの展
開という潔さにも惹かれます。出会った時の想像通りに一般ウケはし
ないのですが、私の中では男らしくも上品な雨合羽のような存在。気
軽に着られる洋服として長く付き合っていきたいと思っています。

In a rare case, I place orders only with my strong desire to wear it,
even though I understand that it would not sell well in stores (laughs).
This cape is such item. The moment I saw it at an exhibition of this
brand, I fell in love with it and intuitively thought, "I definitely want
to own it!" The item has a classic design and a relatively strong
military element, but you can feel the elegance that real military
wear do not have. This is definitely a distinctive charm of Grenfell
that has been stubbornly making in the UK since its establishment
in 1923. It is a one-size-fits-all item, which I like because it captures
the characteristics of a loose cape. As I first imagined it, it's not
popular among ordinary customers, but for me, it's like a manly
and elegant raincoat. This is one of the coats that I can easily wear
without thinking too much. I would like to wear it for a long time.

145

nº 066

HERION,
TURTLENECK T-SHIRT
エリオン、タートルネック T シャツ

product : t-shirt   made in   Italy

material : cotton

20年を経てもいまだに
第一線で活躍しているベテラン選手

A veteran player who has been active on the front line
for 20 years.

長袖のタートルネックカットソーは、どう着るべきか悩む人が多いかも
しれません。でもニットではなく、ある意味で中途半端なアイテムだ
からこそ、スタイリングで醸し出せる独特の味わいがあると思います。
言語化するのは難しいのですが、私自身がおよそ20年前に購入してい
まだに着続けていることが、何よりの証明になるのではないでしょう
か。タートルネックカットソーの中でも特にエリオンが素晴らしいのは、
何年着込んでも伸びず、上品な光沢が失われないこと。いつまでも
新品のような状態を保ってくれるのです。私が所有するカットソーの中
で、トップ3に入る長寿ぶりです。購入当時はレザーを羽織ったカジュ
アルをメインにコーディネートしていましたが、今では季節の変わり目
に、光沢のあるスーツに合わせるなどして楽しんでいます。

Many people may be wondering how to wear a long-sleeved
turtleneck T-shirt. However, because it is not a knit item and is an
uncommon item in a sense, I think it has a unique vibe that can be
created by styling. It is difficult to explain, but I think the best proof
may be that I've worn it for about 20 years. Among such turtleneck
t-shirts, Herion stand out because it still has its elegant luster and
has not stretched out even after years of wearing. It is one of the top
three long-life T-shirts that I own. After I bought it, I mainly styled
it casually such as with a leather jacket, but now I like to style it
with a glossy suit in between-seasons.

Watch & Jewelry Clothing(American) Fashion Accessory Bag Clothing(European) Shoes Others

HERMÈS,
DUFFLE COAT
エルメス、ダッフルコート

product : coat   made in France

material : wool

若い頃に憧れていたモノ
ズバリではないけれど、これが最良

Although it's not exactly what I longed for
when I was young, but this is the best.

エルメスが気になりはじめたのは、クロージングに興味を持つように
なって数年が過ぎた20代半ば頃。アイコンともいえるオレンジカラー
のダッフルコートを「いつかは手に入れたい」と漠然と思っていまし
たが、当時の自分にはまだ似合うはずもなく、断念せざるをえません
でした。それから十数年、私も40歳になり「板につくのはまだ早いか
もしれないけれど、そろそろ片足を突っ込んでみても良い年齢なので
は?」との思いで購入したのが、このダッフルコートです。色は憧れて
いた華やかなオレンジとは違いシックなブラウンですが、上質なカシ
ミアのクルーネックニットにジーンズというラフな装いや仕立ての良いテー
ラードにサラッと合わせるには、これが最良の選択。現存しないムー
アブルック社のエリシアンという生地を使っている点もお気に入りです。

I began to have interests in Hermès in my mid-twenties, a few years
after I became interested in men's dress clothing. I vaguely thought
that I would like to get a duffle coat in orange color, which can be
said to be an icon color of the brand. But it never suited me at that
time, so I had to give up. When I became 40 years old, I thought "It
may be still too early for me to look good in it, but I think I have
reached an age that I can start wearing it." I therefore bought this
duffle coat. The color is chic brown, not the gorgeous orange that I
longed for, but this is the best choice to match items such as quality
cashmere crew neck knit, jeans, and well-tailored jackets. I also like
the fact that it is made of the fabric called Elysian from Moorbrook,
a textile company that does not exist anymore.

IGARASHI TROUSERS, MADE TO MEASURE TROUSERS

五十嵐トラウザーズ、メイド・トゥ・メジャー トラウザーズ

product : trousers

made in : Japan

material : wool

脚を通すたびに気分が高揚する
世界レベルのクオリティ

World-class quality that lifts my spirits every time
I put them on.

このパンツはフルオーダーではなくメイド・トゥ・メジャーによるもの。
日本を代表するパンツ専業ブランド、五十嵐トラウザーズの魅力は、
それで十二分に味わえると私は考えています。生地はドーメル社のヴィ
ンテージスポーテックス。かなり肉厚なのですが、既製品ではあまり
見られない生地で仕立てたいという思いから、これを選びました。た
だし、梳毛を使用しているため比較的軽く滑らかで、3シーズン着用
可能。とても使い勝手に優れています。海外の名だたるパンツ専業ブ
ランドやサルトのものと比べても遜色ないクオリティ、日本人の体型を
熟知している点、独学で学んだ技術……。このブランドの良さは枚挙
にいとまがありません。だからなのでしょう、これに脚を通すたびに、
いつも気持ちが高揚してしまうのは。

These are made-to-measure trousers, not bespoke trousers. By
made-to-measure, you can fully enjoy the charm of Igarashi
Trousers, the Japan's leading brand specializing in trousers. The
fabric is DORMEUIL's vintage SPORTEX. It's quite thick, but I chose
it because I wanted to make the pants with a fabric that is not often
seen in ready-made products. Because it uses worsted fabric, it is
relatively light and smooth, which makes the trousers wearable for
three seasons. There are so many good things about this brand:
the quality is comparable to trousers of famous specialty brands or
sarto; they are familiar with Japanese body shapes; and they learned
many techniques by themselves. Those should be the reasons why I
always feel uplifted when I put my legs through these trousers.

JOHN SMEDLEY, BRADWELL

ジョンスメドレー、ブラッドウェル

product : knit polo shirt

made in England

material : left/wool right/cotton

モテない洋服No.1だけど 男ならこれくらいは着こなしたい

A real man should be able to wear it fashionably, although it is the least appealing item to women.

30ゲージの上質なウールやシーアイランドコットンを使用した、身体に馴染むニットポロ。特筆すべきは、この手のジャンルでは随一といえる襟の美しさです。立体的ゆえジャケットを着るとさらにサマになり、その見栄えの良さは"紳士のためのポロシャツ"という表現がよく似合います。そもそも、ジョンスメドレーのポロシャツに初めて袖を通したのは、クラシックなおじさんに憧れていた20代の頃。背伸びをしてイングリッシュカラーとゆったりとしたサイズ感が特徴の定番モデル、ドーセットを着ていました。似合うかどうかよりも、着たい気持ちを優先させてしまい、結果"着られていた"感じでしたけど……。ようやくここ最近は"モテない洋服No.1"といわれる長袖ポロもサマになる年齢に。昔買ったドーセットも、再び日の目を見る機会が訪れそうです。

These are knit polo shirts that fit your body using 30-gauge high quality wool or Sea Island cotton. It is notable that the shape of the collar is beautiful, which can be said to be the best in this kind. Because the collar is three-dimensional, wearing a jacket makes it even more attractive. It is often called "a polo shirt for gentlemen" because of its nice appearance. I was in my twenties, dreaming to be a well-dressed gentleman, when I first put my arms through the sleeves of John Smedley knit polo shirt. The model that I wore was DORSET, which is a classic model featuring English collars and a relaxed fit. Now looking back myself, I prioritized the feeling of wanting to wear it rather than whether it suits me or not. As a result, I felt like that the DORSET stood out more than I did. Now that I got older, I feel that a long-sleeved knit polo shirt fits me, although it is an item that is said to be the least appealing to women. And DORSET, which I bought in my twenties, is likely to have another chance to see the light of day.

LA FAVOLA, WRAP COAT

ラ ファーヴォラ、ラップコート

product : <u>coat</u> made in <u>Japan</u>

material : <u>cotton</u>

洋服屋だからこそ理解できる
こだわりを詰め込んだコート

A coat packed with special details
that clothiers should understand.

深い前合わせでトレンチコートの前ボタンをなくしたデザイン、限りなく深い背面のインバーテッドプリーツ。このコートには洋服を知っている者こそが理解できるディテールが随所にあしらわれており、洋服屋としてとても心をくすぐられます。中でも、私が特に気に入っているのが袖の作り。袖の上部と脇下の下部で生地2枚を縫いあわせた"2枚袖"を採用しつつ、なで肩で、着ていると肩から自然に抜けるようにカッティングされています。またその袖はユルく、美しく落ちるのです。クラシックでありながらモダンな雰囲気も感じさせる、まさに名品といえる佇まいです。そして、どこかパリっぽい世界観は、デザイナーである平 剛氏ならでは。この未完成のようで完成された洋服は、まるで仕立ての良いスーツを気崩しているかのように着られて、とても気に入っています。

This coat is a design that eliminated the front buttons of the trench coat, and it comes with deep front alignment and deep inverted pleats on its back. In this coat, there are many details that only those who really know clothes understand, which means that this coat is very appealing for clothiers. Of all the good things about this coat, I especially like the sleeve structure. Two pieces of fabric are sewn together to make each sleeves, and the shoulders are sloped. They enables the sleeves to fall loosely and beautifully. This coat has classic yet modern vibes, and the appearance is beautiful enough to be called a true masterpiece. Its Paris-ish impression is something unique to its designer Tsuyoshi Taira. It looks like unfinished, but it's actually a consummate coat, and I can wear it just like I wear a well-tailored suit casually, which is why I love it.

LEWIS LEATHERS,
1970S RIDER'S JACKET ELECTRA

ルイスレザーズ、1970 年代製 ライダーズジャケット エレクトラ

product : rider's jacket　　made in　England

material : sheep leather

イギリスのテーラードジャケットにも
通じる趣がある

It has the taste similar
to British tailored jackets.

ヴィンテージのライダーズジャケットが放つ味わい深さ。アメリカ製のラ
イダーズジャケットとは違った洗練された趣。1970年代に作られたこの
ルイスレザーズのエレクトラには、ラギッドでありながらどこかエレガ
ントな側面も持ち合わせた唯一無二の魅力があります。創業当時より
イギリスのテーラーリング技術が落とし込まれており、驚くほどフィット
感が高いのも特徴。ウエストシェイプはキツめで、身体に自然にピッタ
リと吸い付く感じは、まるで騎士の鎧のような佇まいを感じさせます。
なお、1970年代のシープレザーはかなり分厚く、重量感が半端じゃな
い。まさに、イギリスのテーラードジャケットに通じるクセの強い服だ
と思います。それゆえ、ブラックジーンズなど、この雰囲気に負けない
テイストのアイテムをさらりと合わせるようにしています。

I feel the deep taste of a vintage rider's jacket and a sophisticated
style that is different from the US-made rider's jacket. Released in
the 70s, this Lewis Leathers Electra has a unique charm that is
both rugged and elegant. It is also characterized by a surprisingly
superior fit-feeling thanks to British tailoring technology since
its establishment. The waist shape is tight, and the feeling that it
naturally sticks to the body makes you feel like wearing a knight's
armor. The sheep leather of the 70s is surprisingly thick and heavy.
I think it's very characteristic clothes that are similar to British
tailored jackets. Therefore, I try to simply match items with a taste
that does not spoil the vibes, such as black jeans.

MARGARET HOWELL,
CRICKET SWEATER
マーガレット・ハウエル、クリケットセーター

product : knit pullover　　made in Scotland

material : wool

『炎のランナー』から学んだ
洋服との向き合い方

How to face clothes that I learned
from "Chariots of Fire".

映画『炎のランナー』は、クラシックの教科書といえる素晴らしい作品。1920年前後のイギリス、アメリカの上流階級の学生のスタイリングが凝縮されています。初めて観た30代の頃は洋服ばかりに目が行って、内容が頭にまったく入ってこなかったくらいです。クリケットセーターは、冒頭のシーンから登場します。それに合わせたストライプのブレザーやホワイトフランネルのパンツは現代ではまるで懐古趣味ですが、私は洋服の歴史を学び自分なりに解釈し、常にアップデートさせることを意識しているので、ひとつの指標として参考になります。現代に生きる私たちは、古くからある洋服を少しのアイデアで新しく見せることができる。このスコットランド製のクリケットセーターは、そんな洋服との誠実な向き合い方を思い起こさせてくれる存在なのです。

The movie "Chariots of Fire" is a wonderful work that can be called a textbook of classic styles. The styles of British and American upper class students around 1920 are condensed in this film. When I first saw it in my thirties, I focused on the clothes of the characters too much to remember anything about its story. The cricket sweaters appear from the opening scene. Striped blazer and white flannel trousers look too outdated today, but it is always important for me to learn the history of clothing, interpret it in my own way, and update it accordingly with the current times. So there is no doubt that such items and styles are indicators for me. Today, we can make fresh clothes by updating old ones with a few ideas. This Scottish cricket sweater is a reminder of how to faithfully face clothes.

n° 073

MARINA MILITARE ITALIANA, 1970S VINTAGE KNIT
イタリア海軍、1970年代製 ヴィンテージニット

product : knit pullover   made in Italy

material : wool

洗濯機でラフに洗っても
まったくヘタれない堅牢なニット

Durable knit pullover that does not get shabby
even washed in the washing machine.

ヴィンテージショップで気になるアイテムを見つけた時、私は必ずそれ
をグッと手で握って素材や質感を確かめます。このニットと出会った時
もそう。触れた瞬間にウール100%だということはわかったのですが、
同時に硬くてぬめり感のある風合いから、糸が良いことも窺い知るこ
とができました。こうなったら購入せずにはいられません。いわゆる"買
い"の瞬間ですね。幸いショップで触れた瞬間のファーストインプレッ
ションに間違いはなく、とても堅牢なニットだったので、汚れてもクリ
ーニングには出さずそのまま洗濯機へ放り込むようにしています。それ
でもまったく型崩れしません。洋服屋としては少々雑な印象を持たれ
るかもしれませんが、洗濯などのケアが手軽であることは、間違いな
く私がミリタリーニットを愛する理由のひとつです。

Whenever I find an item in a vintage shop that interests me, I
always grab it with my hand and check the material and texture.
I did the same when I found this. The moment I touched it, I knew
that it was 100% wool, but at the same time, I could see that its
yarns were good because of its hard and a bit slimy texture. When
this happens to me, I cannot leave the store without buying it. It's
the so-called "must buy" moment. Fortunately, the first impression
when I touched it at the shop was right, and it was definitely a very
durable knit pullover. So even if it gets dirty, I don't take it to a
dry cleaner. I just throw it into the washing machine at home. Even if I
do so, it doesn't lose its shape at all. As a clothier, it may sound a bit
careless, but the ease of laundry and other care is definitely one of
the reasons why I love military knitwear.

RING JACKET,
HAND LINE SUIT
リングヂャケット、ハンドラインスーツ

product : suit .... made in Japan ....

material : wool ....

構想20年でようやく完成した
理想のフィレンツェスタイルスーツ

20 years of conception.
The ideal Florentine style suit finally completed.

大学時代、アルバイト先でリヴェラーノ＆リヴェラーノに代表されるフィレンツェスタイルのスーツに初めて袖を通しました。私がいまだにこのスタイルに憧れを抱いたり懐かしさを覚えたりするのは、その時の感動が忘れられないからだと思います。このスーツは、そんなフィレンツェスタイルに対する感動を今の時代に即した形で提案できたら面白いかも、との思いから国内有数のテーラーリングの技術を誇るリングヂャケットとともに作りました。使用したのは、テイラー＆ロッジの中でも最上級の羊毛のみで織り上げたラムズゴールデンベールという生地。密度があり、ハリとコシとツヤ、そしてドレープ感があるのが特徴です。周りの人には新鮮、私にとってはどこか懐かしい。ある意味20年近い構想期間を経てようやく完成した、理想の一着です。

When I was a college student, I put on a Florentine style suit, represented by Liverano & Liverano, for the first time at a store where I worked part-time. I still admire this style of suit and feel nostalgic because I can't forget the excitement of wearing it. I thought it would be interesting if we could propose such Florentine style of suit in a way that suits for today. We therefore made this suit together with Ring Jacket that boasts one of the leading tailoring techniques in Japan. The fabric used is called Lumb's Golden Bale, which is woven only from the finest wool of Taylor & Lodge. It is characterized by its high density, firmness, elasticity, luster, and drape. Most people would feel it is fresh while it makes me feel somewhat nostalgic. In a sense, it is an ideal Florentine style suit that finally completed after 20 years of conception.

SAINT JAMES,OUESSANT
& VINTAGE STRIPED PULLOVER KNIT

セントジェームス、ウエッソン & ヴィンテージボーダーニット

product : ouessant/basque shirt
vintage/marine sweater

made in France

material : ouessant/cotton vintage/wool

8分袖のボーダーには
タイムレスな魅力がある

Bracelet-length sleeve striped pullovers
have timeless appeal.

ブランド定番のバスクシャツ、ウエッソン（写真右上以外すべて）は、
高校時代に初めて購入したのですが、お店で試着しなかったこともあ
り、洗ううちに生地が縮んでピチピチの状態で着続けたという苦い記
憶が（笑）。たしかに洗うと縮みますが、その分、生地が堅牢でガシ
ガシとラフに着られる良さがあります。5年ほど前に購入した白×紺の
ボーダー柄は、長年洗って着込むほどに紺が良い感じに褪せてきまし
た。この経年変化も"味"として楽しめます。一方、1960年代に作られ
たボーダーニット（右上）は、今も展開のあるモデル、ビニック Ⅱの原型。
船乗りの海上での防寒用に作られた、強撚糸による厚手のウールニッ
トです。いずれも船上での作業中に袖が濡れにくいように設定された8
分袖。こういった背景のあるディテールもお気に入りです。

I bought the classic Basque shirt, ouessant (all except the one on
the right in the photo), for the first time when I was a high school
student. I couldn't try it on at the store, and the fabric shrank as I
washed it, so I kept wearing it small... (laughs). Certainly it shrinks
when washed, but the fabric is tough and you can casually wear it
for years. About the white x navy striped ouessant that I bought
about 5 years ago, the navy color has faded nicely after being worn
and washed for years. I think this is a wonderful item that you can
enjoy such changes as "aging" over time. On the other hand, the
striped knit pullover made in the 60s is the prototype of the model
"BINIC II" that is still on sale. It's a thick wool knit pullover made
of strong twisted yarns, designed to be worn by sailors on the sea
to protect against the cold. All bracelet-length sleeves are set to
prevent the sleeves from getting wet while working on board. I like
such details and interesting stories behind them.

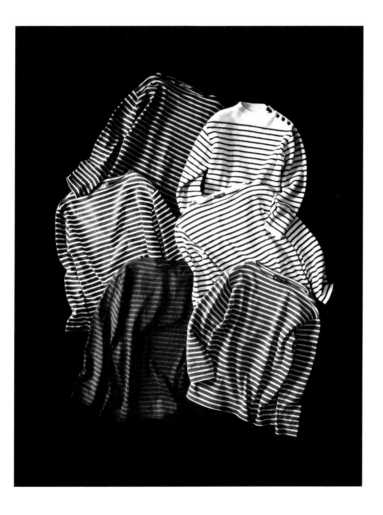

n° 076

SEALUP,
TIELOCKEN COAT

シーラップ、タイロッケンコート

product : coat   made in Italy

material : linen × cotton × polyurethane

年に数回しか着られない
コートがくれる心のゆとり

A coat that can be worn only a few times a year
gives me a sense of comfort.

数々のビッグメゾンのコートを手がけるシーラップが、トレンチコートの
原型ともいわれているタイロッケンコートをベースに作った一着。ボタ
ンが表から見えないフライフロント仕様になっているため、ベルトだけ
で締めているように見え、程良いユルさを演出できるのが特徴です。
セットインスリーブながらシルエットはほんのりAラインになっており、
上品かつモダン。コートなのに素材にはポリウレタン加工を施したリネ
ンが使われているため、実は夏くらいしか着られないのですが、着用
できる期間が短いからこそ味わえる贅沢感は、何ものにも代え難い。
季節に応じて洋服を変えるのはごく当たり前のことですが、移り変わ
る四季の中で、年に数回しか着られない洋服を所有する喜びもあるの
です。この特別感は、自分自身の心のゆとりにもつながると思います。

Sealup, which manufactures coats for many luxury brands, made
this coat, based on a tielocken coat, which is said to be the prototype
of a trench coat. Thanks to its fly-front that hides front buttons, it
looks like it is tightened only with a belt, which creates moderately
loosen look. Although it has set-in sleeves, the silhouette is slightly
A-line, which looks elegant and modern. Although it's a coat,
polyurethane-processed linen is used as the material, so it can only
be worn in the summer. The luxury feeling when you enjoy such
coat for a short period of time a year is irreplaceable. We change
clothes according to the seasons, but it is also a pleasure to own this
coat that I can wear only a few times a year. I think that this special
feeling relaxes my mind.

STILE LATINO,
DENIM DOUBLE BREASTED JACKET

スティレ ラティーノ、デニム製 ダブルブレストジャケット

product : jacket

made in Italy

material : wool × cotton

"既製服の天才"が作った
誰でも格好良くなれるダブルブレスト

Double-breasted jacket made by "genius of ready-made clothes" that makes anyone look cool.

私が愛するテーラードブランドのひとつであるスティレ ラティーノの最大の魅力は、独特な色気を備えたダブルブレストにあります。事実、所有しているラティーノのスーツやジャケットの7割がダブル合わせ。そして、このデニムジャケットも、例に漏れずダブルブレストです。素晴らしい点はいくつもありますが、このブランドの襟の表情はまさしく唯一無二。ダイナミックなのに決して奇抜には見えないところに、不思議な色気を感じます。それをこだわりの生地（こちらはウールコットンによるデニム）や卓越したパターンと組み合わせることで、誰が着ても格好良く見える一着が完成するのです。これこそが、"既製服の天才"といわれるヴィンチェンツォ・アットリーニ氏が作る服の真骨頂。一般的な既製服ブランドでは到達できない領域の逸品だと思います。

One of the tailoring brands I love, Stile Latino's greatest appeal is its double-breasted jacket with unique attractiveness. In fact, 70% of my Stile Latino suits and jackets are double-breasted including this denim jacket. There are many great points, but the appearance of the collar unique to this brand is truly one-and-only. I feel mysterious attractiveness in the point that it is dynamic but never look showy. By combining it with a carefully-chosen fabric (this is denim made of wool and cotton) and an outstanding pattern, Stile Latino creates a piece that looks cool no matter who wears it. This is the true value of clothes made by Vincenzo Attolini, a "genius of ready-made clothes". I think it is a gem that exists in the area where normal ready-made clothing brands cannot reach.

☐ Watch & Jewelry ☐ Clothing(American) ☐ Fashion Accessory ☐ Bag ☒ Clothing(European) ☐ Shoes ☐ Others

STILE LATINO,
POLO COAT

スティレ ラティーノ、ポロコート

product : coat   made in Italy

material : wool

人を惹きつける色気をまとった
素晴らしきテーラードコート

A wonderful tailored coat
with an irresistible appeal.

今から15年ほど前。イタリア・フィレンツェで開催のメンズファッション見本市「ピッティ・イマージネ・ウオモ」に初めて同行させてもらった時に、尊敬する上司が着ていたのがスティレ ラティーノのコートです。立体的で美しく、上品で男らしい色気をまとった独特の雰囲気にひと目で魅了され、思わず「どこのコートですか?」と聞いてしまったのを覚えています。その数年後、このコートを着て、アシスタントバイヤーとして再びピッティへ。ブランドの代表であるヴィンチェンツォ・アットリーニ氏本人から、「良いコートを着ているな」と笑顔で褒めていただいたのは良い思い出です。そして私がディレクターという立場になった現在も、このコートとはもちろん、憧れのヴィンチェンツォ氏とも良い関係が続いているのは、とても感慨深く幸せなことだなと思います。

It was about 15 years ago. When I first accompanied with buyers to the men's fashion trade fair "Pitti Immagine Uomo" in Florence, Italy, my boss I respected wore a Stile Latino coat. I still remember being fascinated by the unique vibes of three-dimensional, beautiful, elegant and masculine appeal, and I couldn't resist asking him "What is the coat you are wearing now?" A few years later, I wore this coat and went back to Pitti as an assistant buyer. It was a very good memory that Vincenzo Attolini, the representative of the brand, gave me a compliment with a smile, "That's a nice coat." And even now that I am in the position of fashion director, I feel deeply honored and happy to keep a good relationship with Mr. Attolini, who I respect and long for, as well as with this coat.

nº 079
—
nº 093

Shoes

価格は履き心地の良し悪しに
直結するものではありません
The price does not affect
comfort to wear.

n⁰ 079

ALDEN,
CORDOVAN TASSEL LOAFERS
オールデン、コードバン製タッセルローファー

product : loafers .... made in U.S.A. ....

material : cordovan ....

もっともオールデンらしさを感じられる
万能なローファー

Versatile loafers
that are quintessentially Alden.

私が初めてオールデンのタッセルローファーを購入したのは大学時代。
そのモデルはカーフ製で、履き潰してから後輩に譲ってしまいました。
その後、どうしてもオールデンの代名詞であるコードバン製のものが
欲しくなり、こちらを購入。紐靴感覚で履ける唯一のローファーとし
て、スーツからカジュアルまで合わせられて本当に万能です。もちろん、
コードバンは水に弱いので、雨が降らない日限定ですが。ちなみに私
の足には、オールデンのアバディーンラストのDウィズが非常によく合
います。これまで世界各国の様々な靴を履いてきましたが、その中で
も「これが一番フィットしている！」と思えるほど快適です。まっすぐな
形のラストからはイギリスを意識していることも垣間見えて実にエレガ
ント。もっともオールデンらしさが感じられる一足です。

I first bought Alden tassel loafers when I was in college. Those were
made of calf leather, but I gave them to my younger friend after
wearing them out. After that, I really wanted the same model made
of cordovan, which is synonymous with Alden, and I bought them
later. As the only loafers that can be worn like lace shoes, they are
truly versatile shoes that can be styled with a range of clothes from
suits to casual clothes. Of course, cordovan is vulnerable to water,
so I only wear them when it does not rain. By the way, Alden's shoes
with Aberdeen Last and D width fit my feet very well. I have worn
a variety of shoes from all over the world, but when I wear them,
I think, "These fittings are the best!" The last is straight in shape,
which shows Alden's awareness of British design. As they are very
elegant, they are quintessentially Alden.

BAUDOIN & LANGE, BELGIAN SHOES

ボードイン & ランジ、ベルジャンシューズ

product : loafers .... made in England ....

material : goat suede ....

究極にラグジュアリーなのに
独特のユルさもあるイギリス靴

Luxurious yet uniquely effortless
British shoes.

決して丈夫とは言えませんが、繊細さや品の良さにおいては唯一無二。イタリア靴にはない、イギリス靴らしい高貴さを感じさせるのが、このボードイン & ランジのベルジャンシューズです。デザイナーのアラン・ボードイン氏は「タキシードからジェットセッターまで、どんなスタイルに合わせても成立する究極のラグジュアリーな靴」と語っていますが、まさにその通りだと思います。カジュアルスタイルをドレスアップしてくれ、ドレススタイルには柔らかさを与えてくれます。ちなみに以前、アラン氏本人に「Apple社のエグゼクティブを務めていたのに、なぜ靴を作るようになったの?」と尋ねると、「パソコン見すぎてしんどくなった」との答えが。そんな、育ちの良い人間ならではの大らかな雰囲気が、この靴にもそのまま反映されていると思います。

You can never say they are tough, but their exquisiteness and elegance are truly unique. These BAUDOIN & LANGE Belgian shoes have the British nobility that Italian shoes rarely have. The designer Allan Baudoin says, "They are the ultimate luxury shoes for any style, from tuxedo to jet setters." and I think that's exactly what they are. They dress up your casual style and give your dress style some softness. When I asked Allan himself, "Why did you start making shoes though you were an executive of Apple?" He answered "I got tired of looking at computers." I think his heartwarming character is reflected to these shoes.

CONVERSE,
ALL STAR J HI
コンバース、オールスター J HI

product : <u>sneakers</u> made in <u>Japan</u>

material : <u>canvas</u>

自分の人生のファッションシーンを
彩ってきた一足

A pair of shoes
that colored my life of fashion.

コンバースのオールスターは、人生の中で一番付き合いが長い靴。初めて履いたのは、小学校の高学年の頃でした。その後、中高時代は学ランに白もしくは黒のモデルを合わせるなど、約30年間途切れることなくずっと愛用しています。この靴とともに思い出を刻んできたと言っても過言ではなく、"自分の人生のファッションシーンを彩ってきた一足"であることは間違いありません。この靴に初めて出会った頃はアメリカ製のものがまだ市場に溢れていましたが、それもいつの間にかなくなり中国製に切り替わってしまいました。数年前、クオリティの高い日本製が出たのを機に、すべてを日本製にシフトしました。ジャケットスタイルに取り入れたり、ライダーズに合わせて1980〜90年代のミュージックシーンのような空気感を出したりするのが今の気分です。

Converse ALL STAR is the shoe I've worn for the longest time in my life. I first wore them when I was in the upper grades of elementary school. In junior high and high schools, I wore the white or black model with my school uniform, and I've been wearing them for over 30 years. I have carved my memories with these shoes, and there is no doubt that "they have colored my life of fashion." When I first met these shoes, there were still a lot of American-made All Star in the market, but at some point, they became Chinese-made. A few years ago, however, Japan began to produce high quality Converse, so I switched over to it. I like styling it into a jacket or rider's jacket, to visualize the mood of the 80s to the 90s music scene.

n° 082

CONVERSE, U.S. ARMY MODEL
コンバース、アメリカ陸軍支給モデル

product : sneakers   made in U.S.A.

material : canvas

消えたコンバース表記は
20年以上ともに歩んできた証

The Converse label that had all but disappeared
has been with me for over 20 years.

通称"アーミーコンバース"は、その名前が示す通り1970〜80年代にアメリカ陸軍にトレーニング用として納入されていたモデル。素材は無漂白。綿花の色をしており、素朴な空気感が漂います。今、こういうスニーカーはないと思えるほどに古き良きアメリカを体現していて、ラルフ ローレンやアメリカのミリタリーモノとの相性が抜群。エルメスのダッフルコートにヴィンテージデニムを合わせ、その足元にサラッと取り入れるのも好きです。この"アーミーコンバース"は、たしか男性ファッション誌『Boon』で初めて目にし、大阪のアメリカ村の古着店で見つけました。大学時代の話ですから、かれこれ20年以上履き続けています。デッドストックで購入したため当時はインソールのかかと部分に印字でコンバースの表記がありましたが、今では消えてしまいました。

Known as "Army Converse", it was delivered to the US military
as a training shoe in the 70s and the 80s. The material is totally
unbleached, which leads to the natural cotton color and a rustic
mood. I like the good old American mood of this sneaker, and it
goes well with Ralph Lauren and American military wears. I also
like to coordinate it with my duffle coat of Hermès and a pair of
vintage denim pants. The first time I saw this "Army Converse" was
in the men's fashion magazine "Boon", and found it at a vintage shop
in America-mura, Osaka. This story comes from my college days, so
I have been wearing it for over 20 years. There was a Converse label
on the insole when I bought it as a dead-stock, but it's gone now.

CROCKETT & JONES,
BUTTERFLY LOAFER BRIMSTONE

クロケット＆ジョーンズ、バタフライローファー ブリムストーン

product : loafers   made in England

material : calf leather

エレガントな装いに合わせたい
ドレッシーなローファー

Dressy loafers for an elegant look.

ロンドン出張の際、メンズウェアの老舗ブランド、ニュー＆リングウッドのショーウィンドウに飾られたローファーがキラキラと輝いて見えました。調べてみると、ベースとなったのはクロケット＆ジョーンズの1930年代のビスポークデザインで、90年代からニュー＆リングウッドの定番靴としてクロケットに製作を依頼したモデルのよう。モカにブローギングとパーフォレーションが施され、クロスしたサドル部が蝶のように見えることからバタフライローファーと呼ばれています。ローファーでありながらドレッシーなイメージを備えており、個人的には紐靴と同じような用途。スーツの時にこそ美しく収まる一足だと思います。ローファーの語源は"怠け者"とされていますが、怠け者には到底履きこなすことができないエレガントなローファーなのです。

When I was on a business trip to London, a brilliant pair of loafers was displayed in the show window of the well-established menswear brand New & Lingwood. I found out that it was the model that was based on Crockett & Jones' bespoke design in the 1930s. Moreover, it seemed to be that New & Lingwood asked Crockett & Jones to make standard shoes for them in the 90s. They are called butterfly loafers, since the brogues and perforations are carved on the moccasin and the crossed saddle looks like a butterfly. Dressy and elegant as they are, butterfly loafers can be worn in the same way as lace-up shoes. I think that they fit suits perfectly. The origin of the word "loafer" is said to come from the word "lazy", but it is an elegant loafer that lazy people can never master.

CROWN,
DANCE SHOES

クラウン、ダンスシューズ

product : lace-up   made in   England

material : cow leather

白の革靴では間違いなく
3本の指に入る名品

White leather shoes
ranked among the top three of all.

ゴム底でインソールにクッション性があり、アッパーのレザーも柔らかいため、履き心地は本当に快適。さらに、アッパーは汚れにくく、雨の日にも履くことができる。白の革靴なのに日常的に履ける一足として愛用しているのが、このクラウンのダンスシューズです。イギリスのシューズブランドでありながら絶妙なヌケ感があるので、フレンチっぽい雰囲気で履きこなせるところもお気に入り。まさにスニーカー以上革靴未満という塩梅です。力が抜けていながらシックに見えて、放つオーラは紛れもなく一級品。これを履くだけで洒落っ気をさり気なく演出できるのが魅力ですね。定番靴だから、もし履き潰してしまってもまた買い直して一生履き続けたい。大人の男に似合う白の革靴においては、確実に3本の指に入る名品だと思います。

The cushioning of the insoles and the soft leather uppers make this shoe really comfortable to wear. In addition, the upper leather is stain resistant so the shoes can be worn even on rainy days. Despite the color, I wear these CROWN dance shoes on a daily basis. It is a British brand, which has an exquisite mood and I also like the fact that it can be worn with a French taste. It's like a pair of shoes that is between a sneaker and a leather shoe. Despite the relaxing look, these are truly stylish and undoubtedly a first-class product. Just by coordinating these shoes, you can casually produce a fashionable look. Even if I wear them out, I want to buy another one and keep wearing the same style for the rest of my life. I think it is a real masterpiece and one of the three best white leather shoes for gentlemen.

n° 085

ENZO BONAFÈ,
IMITATION BROGUE SHOES

エンツォ ボナフェ、イミテーションブローグシューズ

product : lace-up   made in Italy

material : calf leather

天邪鬼に黒の表革を選び
天邪鬼にフォーマルシーンに合わせる

Contrary to the surrounding opinions,
I chose black leather, and match it with the formal scene.

このエンツォ ボナフェは、私にとって初めての9分仕立てによるハンド
ソーンの靴。ホールカットと呼ばれる一枚革のアッパーにブローギング
を施しているため、ウイングチップなのにとてもエレガントです。イタリ
ア靴らしく履き馴染みが良く、ソールが減りにくいという点も本当に素
晴らしい。これはソールの素材まで非常に上質なものを使用している
からこそです。完璧なクオリティであることが履いていて実感できます。
購入当時（25歳頃）はイタリアファッション全盛で、周りのショップス
タッフはよく茶靴を履いていましたが、あえて黒の表革を選択。天邪
鬼な私は、「自分はストレートチップに逃げず、ウイングチップをこん
なにドレッシーに履けるんだ」と言わんばかりに、友人の結婚式など
かしこまった席にもキメ靴としてよく履いて行ったのを覚えています。

These Enzo Bonafè shoes are my first hand-sewn welted shoes.
Though they are wing-tipped shoes, the brogues are carved into
single whole-cut leather, and that makes it look extremely elegant.
Like other Italian shoes, these shoes offer a great fit from the first,
and their durable outsoles are really wonderful. Moreover, these
attractive points result from high quality materials. When you wear
these shoes, I guarantee that you can also feel the greatest quality.
At the time when I bought them (around 25 years old), Italian
fashion was at peak. Shop staff around me often wore brown shoes,
but I chose black ones. I remember putting them on at my friend's
wedding ceremony as if showing off my dressy style. I dared not
wear straight-tipped shoes for formal occasions just to be perverse.

□ Watch & Jewelry   □ Clothing(American)   □ Fashion Accessory   □ Bag   □ Clothing(European)   ✓ Shoes   □ Others

n° 086

GRENSON,
COMBINATION FULL BROGUE SHOES

グレンソン、コンビネーションフルブローグシューズ

product : lace-up   made in   England

material : calf leather × cotton

モノ作りの過程に
敬意を表したくなるコンビ靴

Spectator shoes that make you want to pay homage
to the manufacturing processes.

コンビシューズは古い映画の様々なシーンで登場します。黒や茶に白
という配色がもっとも一般的ですが、そういった配色はやや懐古趣味
な感じ。しかしこちらは、コットンとレザー、そしてカーキとミディアム
ブラウンという素材と色のコントラストが秀逸で、むしろモダンな雰囲
気です。1990年代、すでに既製靴として売られていたというそのセン
スの良さには痺れましたね。私は長年モノ作りに関わっているせいか、
モノと対峙した瞬間に、その背景でどれだけ試行錯誤されているのか
を考えてしまうクセがあります。そして、考えるうちに、完成するまで
のプロセスや込められた想いが、おぼろげながら見えることがありま
す。私にとってグレンソンの靴は、まさにそんな一足。よくタイドアッ
プしたコットンやリネンのスーツに合わせています。

Spectator shoes appear in various scenes of old movies. The most
common color scheme is black or brown with white, but such a color
scheme feels a little nostalgic. Contrasts of cotton and leather, and
khaki and medium brown are excellent, making the pair of shoes
look rather modern. These look rather modern. I was carried away
by the good taste that was already sold in this combination as
ready-made shoes in the 90s. Perhaps because I have been involved
in design and manufacturing for many years, the moment I face a
product, I have a habit of thinking about how much trial and error
was done for it to be made. And I sometimes dimly see the process
of making it as well as the creator's thought. For me, Grenson shoes
are exactly like that. I often enjoy matching them with a suit made
of cotton and linen and a tie.

GUCCI,
HORSEBIT LOAFERS
グッチ、ホースビットローファー

product : loafers .... made in Italy ....

material : left/calf right/suede ....

ホースビットローファーの
オリジンならではの華やかな空気感
Brilliant vibes unique to
the origin of horsebit loafers.

グッチのホースビットローファーは、メンズクラシックのマストアイテム。フレッド・アステアなどのウェルドレッサーたちに愛された歴史や、1990年代バブル期の良い意味での華やかな空気感など、その良さを挙げればキリがありません。このローファーの魅力に気づいたのは、ヴィンテージミックススタイルを良いなと思いはじめた8年ほど前。すでに廃盤となっていたスエードのモデル（写真右）を古着店で見つけた時でした。当時、クラシック畑の人間たちが考える靴はグッドイヤーウェルト製法一辺倒だったのですが、マッケイ製法ならではの華奢な佇まいに惹かれたのです。カジュアルスタイルをドレスアップしてくれるだけでなく、ドレススタイルに合わせても嫌味のない色気を演出してくれる。独特の華やかさを備えた特別な一足だと思います。

Gucci's Horsebit Loafers are a must-have for men's classic styles. There is no end if we mentioned good things about them such as the history of being loved by well-dressers such as Fred Astaire and the gorgeous vibes under the Japan's "bubble economy period" in the 90s. I realized the appeal of this loafer about eight years ago when I started to like the vintage mix styles. It was when I found a suede model (pictured right) that was already discontinued, at a vintage shop. At that time, most of those who liked classic styles wore Goodyear-welt construction shoes, but I was attracted to the delicate appearance of Blake (McKay) construction. Not only can these loafers dress up your casual style, but also they can give the elegance that is not showy to your dress style. I believe it is a special pair with unique brilliance.

J.M. WESTON,SIGNATURE LOAFER #180 & CHELSEA BOOTS #705

ジェイエムウエストン、シグニチャーローファー #180 & チェルシーブーツ #705

product : loafers & boots　　made in　France

material : calf leather

履きはじめはとにかく痛いが
いずれ心地良い緊張感へと変化

It hurts at the first, but eventually,
it sublimate to a comfortable fit.

ジェイエムウエストンの靴は、足に馴染むまでに挫折する人も多く、"とにかく最初は痛い"ことで知られます。こんなにも履きはじめが痛いといわれている靴は、私が知る限りありません。アッパーは最高級のボックスカーフ、ソールも時間をかけて自然乾燥させた高密度な革を使用しており、馴染むまでに相当な時間を要するのです。それが"ウエストンは苦行"と言われる所以。ただ、その苦行の先には最高の履き心地が待っています。ほかの革靴は靴が自分に馴染んでくるのに対し、ウエストンは靴に自分を合わせていく作業のよう。そこに気位の高いフランス人との接し方にも似た"心地良い緊張"を感じるのです。独特なデザインとフォルムによって形作られた顔立ちはどことなくお坊ちゃん風。そんなところもフランスの上流階級を連想させます。

What I can say about J.M. Weston shoe, is that many people give up wearing it since "it hurts in the first place". As far as I know, there are no other shoes with such pain at your first try. The upper leather is made of a finest box calf and the sole high density leather that has been naturally dried over time, and it takes a considerable amount of time to get used to it. That's the reason why wearing J.M. Weston is called as a penance. Beyond that, however, the best comfort awaits. While other leather shoes gradually come to match you, wearing J.M. Weston is more like a work matching yourself to the shoes. At the same time, I feel a "comfortable tension" that is similar to how I interact with elegant French people. As these shoes are authentic with unique design and form, they somehow remind me of the French upper class.

JOHN LOBB, LOPEZ

ジョンロブ、ロペス

product : loafers .... made in England ....

material : calf leather ....

サッと手入れをするだけで
十分サマになる極上のローファー

The finest loafers that look great
only by a quick care.

20代の頃、お洒落で機知に富んだ上司が、きれいに磨かれ輝いたロペスを職場でよく履いていました。「この人と同じ歳になったら、こんな風にさらりと履いていたいな」と思っていた記憶が、この靴を見るたびに蘇ります。ペニーローファーのデザインなのに、この上なくエレガント。こういうローファーって、意外とほかにはないと思うのです。厳選された最上級のカーフ、熟練職人による丁寧な作り込み。そして、デザインとステッチワークの美しさや、ラウンドトウでありながら少し華奢に見える完成されたラスト。サッと手入れをするだけで十分サマになるのは、それだけの要素を積み重ねた良い靴であることの証です。40歳を機に買ったこのダークオークのロペスも、当時の上司の年齢に近づいて、ようやくさらりと履けるようになってきた気がします。

My stylish and witty boss often wore Lopez at work when I was in my twenties. They were beautifully polished and shining, which was impressive to me. Every time I saw those shoes, I thought, "I want to wear them like that when I become around the same age as him." No matter how you look at Lopez, it's a simple penny loafer design, but it looks extremely elegant. I don't think there is any other loafer like this. It is made of carefully selected top-class calfskin and carefully crafted by skilled craftsmen. It comes with beautiful design and stitch work and has the perfect last that looks delicate despite the round toe. All you need to keep its beauty is just a quick care, which is a proof that it is a good shoe filled with all the necessary elements to be so. Now that I am getting closer to the age of my boss at that time, I feel that I can naturally wear this dark oak colored Lopez which I bought at the age of 40.

LA MANUAL ALPARGATERA, ESPADRILLE

ラ マヌアル アルパルガテラ、エスパドリーユ

product : espadrille .... made in Spain ....

material : cotton ....

着脱のストレスを感じても
なお履きたいと思わせるエスパ

Putting them on and off may be stressful,
but I still want to wear this Espadrilles.

ラ マヌアル アルパルガテラは、ハンドメイドによる伝統的なエスパド
リーユ作りを1940年から続け、あのサルバドール・ダリからも愛され
たブランド。日本ではあまり知られていませんでしたが、ここのエスパ
ドリーユは独特な雰囲気のデザインが魅力的です。また、創業当初よ
りサスティナビリティにこだわり、天然素材やリサイクル素材を使用す
るモノ作りにも共感できます（本モデルのソールにはタイヤの廃材を使
用）。本品は、夏のカジュアルスタイルのアクセントに好適。足首で紐
を縛ると靴が足にホールドされて美しくフィットし、リネンのスーツや
サマーウールのパンツに粋に収まります。正直、土足文化ではない日
本においては脱ぎ履きが面倒に感じることもありますが、そんなスト
レスよりも"履きたい!"を優先したくなる一足です。

La Manual Alpargatera has been making traditional espadrilles
since 1940, and it is a brand that people such as Salvador Dali loved.
Although the brand was not well known in Japan, its espadrilles
are attractive for their unique design. In addition, they have been
committed to sustainability since their establishment. I sympathize
with their way of thinking and how they work, such as using
natural and recycled materials (the sole of this model uses scrap
tires). This product gives you a good accent for casual summer
style. When you tie the laces to your ankles, the shoes perfectly fit
to your feet and they go well with linen suits or summer wool pants.
Wearing them may be stressful in Japan, since its culture dictates
that people put off their shoes when entering a house. But forget
such a stress and put the desire to wear the Espadrilles first.

PARABOOT,
MICHAEL
パラブーツ、ミカエル

product : tyrolean shoes   made in France

material : lisse leather

全天候型で気兼ねなく履ける
高級な雨靴

All-weather luxury boots
that I can casually wear.

パラブーツの存在は20代の頃から知っていましたが、当初はどちらか
というとアメカジ寄りの印象があり、敬遠していました。しかし、食わ
ず嫌いは良くないと思い、取引先の方の紹介をきっかけに購入。自分
なりにブランドのオリジンを考えた時に、シャンボードやウィリアムより
もミカエルだと思い、遅まきながら30代後半で手に入れました。雨天
時にもガンガン履けるので、極端な表現かもしれませんが、私の中で
は"高級な雨靴"という役割です。雨靴ですから手入れはほとんどして
いません。リスレザー特有の白いロウが浮いてきても、あえて気にし
ないようにしています。汚れがついたら拭き取る程度の本当に必要最
低限のケアだけで、手入れをしていないように無骨に見せた方が、こ
の靴本来の野趣溢れた魅力を堪能できると思うのです。

I've known Paraboot since I was in my twenties. However, I avoided
wearing it since I felt like it was too casual American style.
However, I didn't like having a prejudice, so I decided to buy it when
my business partner introduced it to me. When I thought about
the origin of the brand, I thought I should choose Michael rather
than Chambord or William. The first time I bought it, I was in my
late thirties. In my opinion they are luxury rain boots. I therefore
hardly maintain them. Even if the white wax comes up from the
leather, I dare not worry about it. I only try to do the minimum care,
like wiping off some dirt. Anyway, to enjoy the original wildness of
these shoes, I'd rather keep them look rugged.

TONY LAMA,
1990S WESTERN BOOTS
トニーラマ、1990年代製 ウエスタンブーツ

product : boots   made in : U.S.A.

material : buffalo leather

カウボーイの足元を飾った靴は
今も男の二枚目感を演出してくれる

The shoes that decorate cowboys' feet
still make a man look handsome.

ウエスタンブーツは、渋カジの時代に長髪の"不良"といわれる人たち
に愛されたり、1980年代のパリのエミスフェールから端を発したフレ
ンチアイビーで取り入れられたりと、服飾史でしばしばスポットが当て
られてきました。そういった歴史的な背景はもちろん無視できません
が、"どう履きこなしたいか"の方が私にとっては大切。だから、思いの
ままに履くようにしています。このトニーラマのウエスタンブーツの印象
は、とにかく二枚目。ですから、履き方としてはカウボーイがデニム
にクリースを入れて合わせていたように、裾幅の広いパンツにさり気な
く合わせて、気負わず、でも少し高貴な感じにまとめています。履き
心地があまり良くなく、40歳を過ぎた私には長時間の歩行が耐え難い
ほどなのですが、それでも格好良いのでついつい履いてしまうのです。

Western boots are often spotted in the history of clothing. For
example, they were loved by bad boys with long hair during
the Shibu-caji (Shibuya casual) period in Japan, and they were
incorporated in the so-called "French Ivy" style that originated from
the store "Hemisphere" in Paris in the 80s. Of course, such historical
backgrounds cannot be ignored, but "how to wear them stylishly" is
more important to me. That's the reason why I try to wear them as I
want to, without being bundled by past examples. The impression of
this Tony Lama's western boots is so handsome. So, just like cowboys
matched them with creased jeans, I casually match them with pants
with wide hems in a little noble image. As I'm over 40 years old and
they are too uncomfortable to wear for a long time, but they're still so
cool that make me want to wear them again and again.

WALK-OVER,
1990S WHITE BUCKS SHOES
ウォークオーバー、1990年代製 ホワイトバックスシューズ

product : lace-up .... made in U.S.A. ....

material : nubuck ....

美しい見た目と快適な履き心地を
兼備したアメリカ靴

American shoes combining a beautiful look
and a comfortable fit.

アメリカ製のウォークオーバーは、1990年代の半ばに生産中止になっ
てしまいました。ただ、私が大学生の頃はまだデッドストックが売られ
ていて、当時購入したのがこのホワイトバックスです。グッドイヤーウェ
ルト製法なのに武骨になりすぎず、さらに比較的に安価。それだけで
も十分魅力的なのですが、この靴がここまで有名になった一番の理由
は、素晴らしい履き心地にあると考えています。バランス良く完成され
たラストでありながら、当時はDとEのウィズを選ぶことができたので、
様々な足型にフィットしたのです。ちなみにこの手の靴はアイビーやプ
レッピーに合わせるとテイストが揃いすぎて懐古趣味になってしまいま
す。ヨーロッパ的なリゾートスタイルやイタリア的な柔らかいジャケット
スタイルに合わせることが、よりモダンに見せられるコツです。

American-made WALK-OVER was discontinued in the mid 90s.
However, when I was a college student, dead-stocks were still on
sale and I bought these White Buck shoes at that time. Although
they are Goodyear welted, they're not too rugged and the price was
wallet-friendly. That's attractive enough, but I personally think
that the comfort made them famous. Though they were made by a
well-balanced last, I was able to choose between width D and E. If
you coordinate these kinds of shoes with ivy or preppy style, the
taste will be too aligned and nostalgic. I'd say matching them to
European resort style or Italian soft jacket style, would make you
look more modern.

no
094

—

no
100

Others

良い歳の取り方をするため
身体と心のケアをいつも忘れずに

Always remember to take care of
body and mind to age better.

DAVINES,
AUTHENTIC OIL

ダヴィネス、オーセンティック オイル

product : hair oil .... made in Italy ....

程良くヤレた質感に仕上げてくれる
"良い大人の日用品"

"An everyday item for good adults"
that gives my hair a "moderately aged feeling".

40代になると髪にツヤがなくなり、毛が細くなってきます。そして乾燥しやすくなり、キューティクルも徐々に失われ……。そんな髪の悩みを実感しはじめた矢先に、ヘアサロンの方から紹介されたのがダヴィネスのヘアオイルです。私は髪にツヤとうるおいを与えるために、帽子を被る時も含めて毎日必ず使用しています。上品なツヤが出て、キマりすぎず、程良くヤレた雰囲気に仕上がります。1回の使用量はほんの3滴くらいなので、1本でかなり長持ちするのもうれしいですね。また、コンディションが非常に良い時や、疲れやストレスを抱えている時とで微妙に香りの感じ方が変化するので、身体の状態を知るための毎日のルーティンとしても役立っています。同年代の男性に自信を持って勧められる、これぞ"良い大人の日用品"だと思います。

When you are in your 40s, your hairs become dull and thin. Then they become easier to dry, and the cuticles gradually decrease... This Davines hair oil was introduced to me by a hair salon just when I started to realize such hair troubles. I always use it in my daily hair styling, including when I wear a hat, to give my hairs gloss and moisture. The moderately aged look, without being overly textured, is completed thanks to the elegant luster. Since the amount used at a time is only about 3 drops, I am happy that one bottle last a long time. In addition, the way you feel the scent slightly changes depending on my condition, so as a daily routine, I use it to know my health. I think this is "an everyday item for good adults" that I confidently recommend to men in my generation.

MAGLIA FRANCESCO, UMBRELLA

マリアフランチェスコ、傘

product : umbrella .... made in Italy ....

material : polyester × metal × wood ....

雨の日でも街に出かけたくなる
イタリア製の高級傘

A luxury umbrella made in Italy that makes
you want to go out to town even on a rainy day.

クラシックな装いをする人間にとって、傘は非常に重要なアイテムのひとつ。良い傘を持つとスタイルが一気に映えるからです。では、そもそも良い傘の条件とはなんでしょうか？　個人的には、持つだけで開放的な気持ちになり、思わず街に出かけたくなるのが良い傘だと思っています。高級な傘といえば、イギリスではフォックス、イタリアだとこのマリアフランチェスコが有名。イギリスの傘はストイックで厳格なイメージがあるのに対して、イタリアの傘は開放的なイメージです。また、傘をさす習慣がほとんどない前者は畳んである状態の美しさを最も重視するのに対し、この傘は畳んでもさしても美しく、雰囲気があります。ずっしりとした重みからくる「良い傘を持っている」という満足感も、沈みがちな雨の日の気持ちを高揚させてくれるのです。

Umbrellas are one of the most important items for those who wear
classic clothes. If you have a good umbrella, your style would look
great. Now, what would be the conditions for a good umbrella? I think
it should be a good umbrella if just holding it makes you open-minded
and want to go out to town. When it comes to luxury umbrellas,
famous brands are Fox, Brick, and Peerless from the UK and Maria
Francesco from Italy. British umbrellas have stoic and strict image,
while Italian umbrellas have open-minded image. Also, while British
brands place the highest priority on the beauty of the furled state
probably because people have fewer chances to put up an umbrella,
Maria Francesco's umbrellas have beautiful vibes both when they are
furled and spread. The satisfaction of having a good umbrella comes
from its heavy weight, and my mood will lift on a rainy day.

PARGA, HAIR SOAP SOFT

パルガ、ヘアソープ ソフト

product : hair soap — made in Japan

ヘアスタイルは 装いを構成するうえで大事な要素

Hairstyle is one of the elements
that make up the outfit.

髪の薄くなった父親の姿を見ていて、若い頃は「30代くらいまでは薄毛になりたくない!」と思っていました。同時に、「40代になれば自然と渋くなるはずだから、それも悪くないかも」とも。しかしいざ40代になると、自分が想像していたよりもずっと若造で、髪のない自分は想像できませんでした。「まだまだ髪も健康でいたい」という気持ちになった時期に出会ったのが、このシャンプーです。ヘアサロンでプロが使用している製品で、髪に良いのはもちろん、美容師たちの手を肌荒れから守りたいという思いから、アミノ酸等の原料にこだわっているのだそうです。髪はスタイリングを構成する大事な要素。実は、このシャンプーをオススメしてくれたヘアサロンには10年来通い続けていて、いつも自分の着こなしに似合うヘアスタイルも相談しています。

Watching my father's hair thinning, I used to think, "I never want my hair to be thin until my thirties!" At the same time, I thought, "Because I should look matured in my 40s, it may not be bad." However, when I became 40, I felt myself much younger than I had imagined, and I couldn't imagine myself without hair. I came across this shampoo when I felt like "I want to keep my hair healthy." It is a product used by professionals in hair salons, and it is not only good for hair, but also it prevents the hands of hairstylists from having rough skin, thanks to its raw materials such as amino acids. Hair is an important component of styling for me, who styles my hair according to my outfit. Actually, for the last ten years, I have been consulting the same hairstylist for advice on how to match my hairstyle to my fashion style. It was he who introduced me this shampoo.

211

SANTA MARIA NOVELLA, GINESTRA & CALA ROSSA

サンタ・マリア・ノヴェッラ、ジネストラ&カーラ・ロッサ

product : eau de cologne   made in Italy

香水は季節に合わせて
使い分けるのがマイルール

My rule is to use different perfume
according to the season.

サンタ・マリア・ノヴェッラのオーデコロンを購入したきっかけは、「元々
は上流階級が愛用していたモノをその歴史を含めて実際に自分で感
じてみるのも良いのでは?」と思ったからです。初めてフィレンツェの
本店を訪れたのは、2010年の冬のピッティ出張の時。世界最古の薬
局といわれるだけあって風情があり、商品の種類もとても豊富でした。
数あるラインナップの中から「上品で爽やかな香りが良い」と思い、ス
タッフにシトラス系をリクエスト。4〜5種類出してくれたうちのひとつ
が、写真のジネストラです。花のような香りがして、少し色気を感じる
のが特徴です。同年初夏の出張で再訪した際には、カーラ・ロッサ
を購入。こちらは少し薬草っぽくスパイシーな印象。それ以来、春夏
にはカーラ・ロッサ、秋冬にはジネストラと使い分けています。

The reason why I bought the Santa Maria Novella Eau de Cologne
is that I thought it should be a good idea to actually feel the things
that the upper class used to love, including their history. The first
time I visited its flagship store in Florence was when I was on a
business trip to Pitti in the winter in 2010. As it is said to be the
oldest pharmacy in the world, it was very tasteful and had various
merchandises. When choosing a scent from many products, I
thought that "I want something elegant and refreshing." so I asked
the staff to show me something with citrus. He or she brought me
four to five kinds of perfume, one of which was Ginestra in the
photo. It has a floral scent and feels slightly sexy. When I visited
there again on a business trip in the early summer of the same year,
I bought Cala Rossa. It has a little herbal and spicy impression.
Since then, I've been using Cala Rossa in spring and summer season
and Ginestra in fall and winter season.

TOOT,
UNDERWEAR
トゥート、アンダーウェア

product : underwear　　made in Japan

material : cotton × polyurethane

独特のフィッティングは
一度穿いたらクセになる

Unique fitting that makes you addicted
once you wear it.

ぜひ多くの方に一度試して欲しい！　トゥートのアンダーウェアがそう
私に思わせる一番の理由は、立体構造による独特のフィット感にあり
ます。最初は違和感があるかもしれませんが、それが徐々にクセにな
るのです。このブランドは主張の強いデザインの商品が多いですが、
私はその中でできる限りシンプルで無地っぽいデザインを選んでいま
す。アンダーウェアは他人からは見えないものですが、日々の生活の
中で確実に自分の視界に入ってきます。その時に違和感がなく、自
分が自然体でいられるものを選ぶことが大切だと思っているからです。
だから私は、黒っぽい装いの時にアンダーウェアだけ真っ赤なものを
選んだりはしません。人目に触れることはありませんが、洋服の色に
合わせて黒にするのが、私にとっては違和感のない選択なのです。

I really want many people to try it once! The main reason for that
is the unique fit that comes from the three-dimensional structure.
You may feel strange at first, but it gradually becomes addictive.
This brand has many products with strong designs, but I try to
choose the one with the simplest design available. Underwear is
invisible to others, but it definitely comes into your sight in your
daily life. I think it is important for you to choose something that is
comfortable and natural. That's why I do not choose underwear in
bright red when I wear dark clothes, for an example. It's not visible
to others, but it's a natural choice for me to choose black along with
the color of my clothes.

WOW CREAM, FACE CREAM

ワウ クリーム、フェイスクリーム

product : face cream — made in Switzerland

洋服を長く楽しむために 最低限のスキンケアを欠かさない

Bare minimum skincare
to enjoy clothes for a long time.

洋服は、健康な心と身体があってこそ楽しめるもの。自分の好きな洋服と長く付き合っていけるように、30代の頃から風呂上がりに化粧水を顔に塗るなどの最低限のケアをするようにしてきました。ただ、もともと鼻炎や花粉症に悩む私は、化粧水を塗っても肌が荒れてしまうこともしばしば。しかし、最近このオールインワンタイプのクリームを使うようになってからは、吹き出物や肌荒れがほとんどなくなり、肌のコンディションが見違えて良くなったのです。そしてそれにともない、食事などの生活習慣全般にも、より気を遣うようになりました。年齢とともに体調が顔に出やすくなるものですが、私は歳に逆らってまで無理に若作りしようとは思いません。毎朝、毎晩、洗顔後と風呂上がりにこのクリームを塗り、良い歳の重ね方をしていきたいと思っています。

I always think that you cannot fully enjoy the clothes until you have a healthy mind and body. In order to wear my favorite clothes for a long time and to age in a good way, I have been doing minimum skincare since my thirties such as applying lotion to my face after taking a bath since my thirties. Still, since I have rhinitis and hay fever, my skin often got rough even when I applied lotions. However, since I recently started using this all-in-one type cream, my skin condition has improved a lot, with almost no pimples or rough skin. And along with that, I have become more concerned about my lifestyle habits such as eating. As we get older, our physical conditions become more visible, but I don't want to try hard to make myself look younger than my age. I would like to apply this cream on my face every morning, every night, after washing my face, and after taking a bath, and get older in a good way.

nº 100

YARD-O-LED, VICTORIAN

ヤード・オ・レッド、ヴィクトリアン

product : ballpoint pen　　made in England

material : sv925

30歳の記念に手に入れた
洋服屋にとってのペンの理想形

My 30th birthday present:
Clothiers' ideal pen.

入社時、先輩から「洋服の販売員のペンは、お客様に署名してもらう時に差し出すモノだからチープであってはならない」と教えられました。当時はほとんどのスタッフがモンブランかモンテグラッパを使っており、私だけがローズウッドのカランダッシュ。理由は少しスポーティな印象が、ジャケットスタイルが多かった自分には合うと考えていたからです。しかし、販売員としてのペンへの心構えを先輩から聞いて以来、独りよがりな考えを反省し、よりふさわしい一本を探すように。そして30歳の記念に購入したのが、このヤード・オ・レッドのボールペンです。創業以来ハンドメイドを貫く生産背景や、滑らかな書き味、そしてスターリングシルバーと美しい彫刻による高貴な佇まいは、やはり大切なお客様に差し出すにふさわしい逸品だと思います。

When I entered the company that I work for now, my senior told me"We should never use a cheap pen because customers use our pen to sign an order." Most of my colleague at that time used Montblanc or Montegrappa, and I was the only one who was using a Caran d'Ache made of rosewood. I thought that its slightly sporty image would suit me, because I often dressed myself with a jacket not a suit. However, since I heard from my senior about the ideal attitude and pen of clothing staff, I reflected on myself for being selfish and started to look for a better pen. And I bought this Yard-O-Led ballpoint pen to cerebrate my 30th birthday. Since its establishment, the company has produced handmade pens, which are smooth in writing. Also sterling silver and beautiful sculptures form an excellent shape. I think that it is a gem suitable for letting important customers use for their signing.

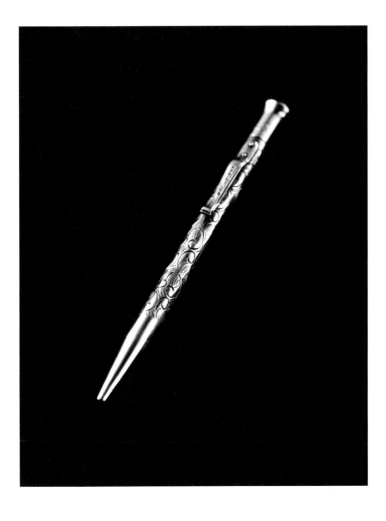

CONCLUSION

本書で紹介した100のアイテムと、それにまつわる人々との
関わりがなければ、今の西口修平は形成されていません。
そういう意味で、どれも私にとっては絶対に欠かせない存在です。
もしかしたら、私以外の大多数の人にとっては、
ほとんどが不要なモノに映るかもしれません。
でも、それで当然——。誰かにとっては価値のあるモノが、
また別の誰かにとってはまったく価値のないモノになる
ダイバーシティな世の中で、
「必要か、不要か?」「価格が高いか、安いか?」
「お洒落か、お洒落でないか?」という二元論で、
モノの価値を測るのはナンセンスですから。
見た目の格好良さにひと目惚れするのもアリですし、
モノの背景にあるストーリーに惹かれることがあっても良い。
大切なのは "自分の物差しでモノを選び、愛すること"。
それを身にまとい、使い込むうちに、スタイルが自然に形成されていく。
毎日がより自分らしく、人生が豊かになっていく。
その喜びを知っていただくお手伝いが本書を通してできたら、
ひとりの洋服屋としてこれ以上の幸せはありません。

メンズファッションディレクター　西口修平

Without the 100 items introduced in this book and the relationships with the people involved, I would not exist as I am. In that sense, they are absolutely indispensable to me. Perhaps, most of them look like unnecessary to the majority of people except for me. But that's natural ... because in this diverse world where something that is valuable to someone is something that is completely worthless to someone else, it is nonsense to judge the value of items in a dualistic way such as "necessary or unnecessary", "expensive or inexpensive", and "stylish or not stylish". You may fall in love with the cool appearance of an item at a first sight, or you may be fascinated by the story behind an item. The most important thing is to be your own master. By wearing or using an item that you chose by yourself, your style forms naturally, every day becomes more personal, and your life becomes richer. If this book could help you to realize such joy, I would not be able to be happier as a clothier.

Men's Fashion Director *Shukei Nishiguchi*

メンズファッションディレクター

西口修平

1977年、大阪府生まれ。古着店やデザイナーズブランドを扱うショップで働いたのち、クラシックに目覚め
大手セレクトショップに入社。関西で約10年間販売職を経験し、バイヤーとして抜擢され上京。2014年よりディレクターを務める。
現在はブランドのディレクションのほか、企業とのコラボレーションやセミナーでの講演などマルチに活動している。

Nishiguchi
Essentials
100

2021年3月16日　第1刷発行

著者／西口修平

発行人／松井謙介

編集人／松村広行

企画編集／青木宏彰

編集執筆／持田慎司

翻訳／深谷翔二、林ジェフリー渓介

撮影／蜂谷哲実(hachiya studio)

スタイリング／稲田一生、水野陽介

校閲／小池晶子(和文)、久保田 遼(英文)

アートディレクション／原田 諭(Hd LAB Inc.)

デザイン／兼光良枝(Hd LAB Inc.)

発行所／株式会社ワン・パブリッシング

　　　　〒110-0005　東京都台東区上野3-24-6

印刷所・製本所／中央精版印刷株式会社

本文DTP／株式会社アド・クレール

●この本に関する各種お問い合わせ先
内容等のお問い合わせは、下記サイトのお問い合わせフォーム
よりお願いします。

不良品(落丁、乱丁)については　☎ 0570-092555
業務センター　〒354-0045　埼玉県入間郡三芳町上富279-1

在庫・注文については書店専用受注センター　☎ 0570-000346

©ONE PUBLISHING

ワン・パブリッシングの書籍・雑誌についての新刊情報・詳細情
報は、下記をご覧ください。
https://one-publishing.co.jp/